SpringerBriefs in Computer Science

More information about this series at http://www.springer.com/series/10028

Orit Hazzan · Yael Dubinsky

Agile Anywhere

Essays on Agile Projects and Beyond

Orit Hazzan
Technion—Israel Institute of Technology
Haifa
Israel

Yael Dubinsky
IBM Research
Haifa
Israel

ISSN 2191-5768 ISSN 2191-5776 (electronic)
ISBN 978-3-319-10156-9 ISBN 978-3-319-10157-6 (eBook)
DOI 10.1007/978-3-319-10157-6

Library of Congress Control Number: 2014947131

Springer Cham Heidelberg New York Dordrecht London

Printed on acid-free paper

Springer is part of Springer Science+Business Media (www.springer.com)

Contents

Chapter 1
Introduction to Agile Anywhere

Abstract We wish to be more agile. Agility is a concept that people, teams, organizations wish to be proud of as one of their traits. The message we convey in this book is that agility can be implemented anywhere, and accordingly, we present ten guidelines for the adoption of agility that enable to cope with changes in our life, in our team, in our organizations. Since we advocate agility, we publish *Agile Anywhere* as a *Springer Briefs*, which includes concise standalone chapters that enable the readership to focus on the specific topic they wish to adopt in order to become agile.

Keywords Agile · Agility · Teams · Organization · Guidelines · Change

1.1 Agile Guidelines

Based on our experience of about 12 years of implementing agile practices in different projects and organizations, as well as in our daily life, we present ten agile guidelines for agile lifestyle to cope with change. We categorize them into three groups: characteristics, behavior, and emotions.

Change characteristics

1. *Time*. Change/improvement takes time; you cannot accelerate it. There is a vision to achieve and a way to go; it takes time to understand the needed process and to apply it.
2. *Stability*. In order to pursue a change process, a stable infrastructure is needed; a change process cannot be initiated in a mess.
3. *Pace*. Complex changes are achieved based on small changes; the complexity of a change process is increased by small changes.
4. *Scope*. Effect spreads in stages like a stone thrown into a lake; at the beginning the change is local; gradually, the radius of the effect cycles of the change increases.

O. Hazzan and Y. Dubinsky, *Agile Anywhere*, SpringerBriefs in Computer Science,
DOI 10.1007/978-3-319-10157-6_1

Behavior while changing

5. *Generative.* Only one thing (can be composed of several smaller things) changes at a time; keep all the other things constant to highlight the current change, its effect, and how to proceed.
6. *Reflective.* Summary and reflection are needed before proceeding to the next change; they are part of the change process and should not be skipped.
7. *Corrective.* Avoidance of harm effects; welcome the identification of deviations, mistakes, misconceptions earlier as possible, and manage their risk.

Change emotions

8. *Trust.* Clarity and transparency deliver quality and foster trust; people trust you when the process is managed professionally and the environment supports the continuation of the change process.
9. *Feedback.* Feedback is important; pain should be conceived as a positive signal since it indicates where a change is needed.
10. *Confidence.* Do not worry (and even enjoy) from uncertainty and unexpected events—they are the basic key and indicators of a successful change.

As we see in this book, we cope with change in a wide range of situations: from daily general-purpose tasks to complex system development projects. The agile guidelines enable us to plan and analyze change processes and steer our route by joining the change.

Chapter 2
From First to Second Edition

Abstract In the introductory chapter of the first edition of this book, published in 2008, we asked questions such as what is agile software development? Why is an agile perspective at software engineering needed? What are the main characteristics of agile software development? What can be achieved by agile software development processes? Does agile software development form a pleasant and professional software development environment? Such questions are now irrelevant since during the past decade, agile software development has become a mainstream approach for managing software development processes. A new trend we witnessed recently is agility anywhere—in many organizations, agility is used today in many areas, not only in software development processes. This is the message of this Brief. We highlight the perspective that agility is not limited anymore to software projects, but rather, it is a lifestyle. Therefore, we decided to call the second edition of our book *Agile Anywhere*. In this chapter, we present our Human–Organizational–Technological (HOT) framework which we extensively used in our first edition and show how it also fits the *Agile Anywhere* point of view (Hazzan and Dubinsky 2010); specifically, by replacing Technological with Thematic, the HOT framework deals with all change scenes (software, human resources, research, education, climate, and more). We illustrate this idea using the theme of education and analyze the Finnish education system, known to be one of the best in the world, from the agile perspective.

Keywords Agile software engineering · Agile environments · Agility anywhere · Agile projects · Agile lifestyle · Human–Organizational–Technological framework · Human resources · Research · Education · Finnish education system

2.1 Three Perspectives of Software Engineering

Software engineering is the profession that applies scientific knowledge in the construction of software products needed by customers. The scientific knowledge in the case of software engineering is mathematics, computer science, and the specific domain that the developed software deals with. In order to achieve their targets,

O. Hazzan and Y. Dubinsky, *Agile Anywhere*, SpringerBriefs in Computer Science,
DOI 10.1007/978-3-319-10157-6_2

software practitioners should be provided with professional tools for how to apply their knowledge. Different approaches toward the application of software engineering processes exist; among them, *Agile Anywhere* focuses on the agile approach.

One of the basic tools that practitioners need in order to accomplish their task is a well-defined engineering process laid out by a software development method. A software development method is a set of activities and practices, as well as roles and norms of behavior, derived from a set of professional aims, which are carried out in a logical and specified order.

A software development method should address not only technological aspects, but rather, it should refer also to the work environment and the professional framework. Accordingly, agile software engineering is reviewed in our book *Agile Software Engineering* (Hazzan and Dubinsky 2008) within the HOT framework by following the three perspectives given below:

- The **H**uman perspective, which includes cognitive and social aspects and refers to learning and interpersonal (teammates, customers, management) processes.
- The **O**rganizational perspective, which includes managerial and cultural aspects and refers to the workspace and issues that spread beyond the team.
- The **T**echnological perspective, which includes practical and technical aspects and refers to how-to and code-related issues.

Specifically, we explain how the attention that agile software development gives these aspects helps coping with challenges of software projects. Figure 2.1 presents schematically the HOT analysis framework in the theme of software engineering.

Following our *Agile Anywhere* approach, we updated this framework to be Human–Organizational–Thematic (HOT) framework which can be applied to all projects with any theme, e.g., technology, education, discipline (e.g., medical, mechanics), and research, as shown in Fig. 2.2.

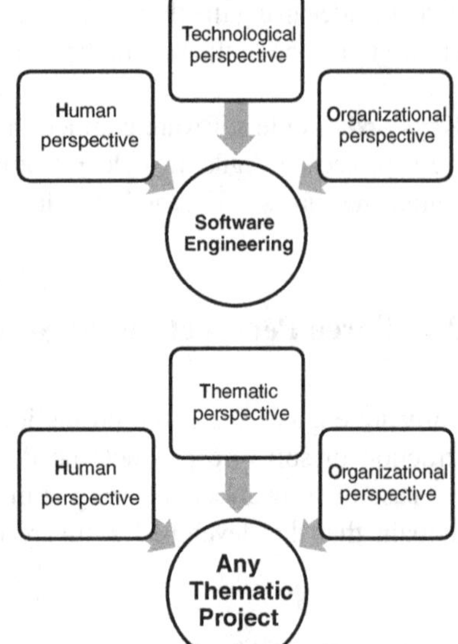

Fig. 2.1 The HOT analysis framework for software engineering (as in our first edition)

Fig. 2.2 The HOT analysis framework for any theme

2.2 Education in Finland from the *Agile Anywhere* Perspective

The Finnish education is known to be one of the best in the world. In this section, we show how the Finnish education system is managed as an agile project. Specifically, we illustrate some of the principles of the Finnish education system from the agile perspective according to the above three perspectives: Human, Organizational, and Thematic. In addition, we ask whether the success of the Finnish education system can be explained by the claim that it applies agile principles.

2.2.1 Thematic Perspective

Teachers as researchers: Finnish teachers are committed to a continuous improvement of teaching. Thus, they spend only a few hours per day teaching, and during the remaining hours of their work day, engage in research, self-examination, reflective processes, and preparation for the next day. This organization of the work day also enables teachers to complete their school work at school, and so they do not have to continue working at home. The agile approach involves a similar process: Working time itself is restricted to a certain number of hours per day that are utilized in an optimal manner. The rest of the time is spent for learning, analyzing the process, and conducting reflective processes in which the team analyzes both the process itself and ways to improve it.

Peer teaching: Part of the learning process in Finland is conducted by students who teach other students, so that the teachers are not, in fact, the sole and main source of knowledge. This is the case in agile projects as well: Each and every member of the team specializes in a certain subject or area and teaches it to the other team members so that all team members are both learners and teachers. In other words, mechanisms exist both in the Finnish education system and in agile environments that support the sharing and management of knowledge, whereby the students (in Finnish schools) and team members (in agile projects) share their knowledge with their peers.

Team work: Team work is one of the basic principles of Finnish education; it is also one of the basic principles of the agile approach. The entire team sits in a single room that contains all of the information required for the project. It seems that this teaching method enables the Finnish education system to turn the profession of teaching, from an "industrial" profession that is based on imparting a certain amount of material within a certain number of hours to as many students as possible, into a profession that is more "clinical" in nature, in which each student receives a greater amount of personal attention.

2.2.2 Organizational Perspective

Fewer school hours: Children in Finland spend fewer hours at school than do children in many other Western countries, yet they achieve better results. These results are apparently attained by utilizing the school hours in a way that encourages significant learning processes. Indeed, it is apparent that in Finland, students are active, they improve their skills, and they teach each other in classes of 15 students and two teachers—another feature that enables the teachers to give each student more personal attention. This is also the situation in agile projects. Efficient time management in agile environments supports the production of higher-quality deliverables in a limited, relatively smaller number of working hours per day, as opposed to the practice of working long hours under other management methods.

Self-managed teams: In Finland, the teachers determine how to achieve the objectives of the education system and develop curricula designed to attain these goals; the education system provides them with the required means to do so. Agile teams conduct themselves in a similar manner: The objectives are defined, but the manner in which tasks are allocated and the course of the process itself are not pre-dictated. In other words, the teams manage themselves. This concept is based on the working assumption that team members are professionals and that their work does not need to be supervised. In Finland, teachers do not need to be supervised either. This approach, which eliminates the supervision tier and minimizes administration and bureaucracy, enables to better utilize resources. In Finland, this is manifested also in social justice, small social gaps, and a society that grants everyone the same right to education.

Early identification of problems: In Finnish education, this concept refers to the early identification of struggling students who are then allocated special resources. This approach enables problems to be addressed before they are aggravated and require even greater resources. Early identification of problems is also one of the more important principles of the agile approach and is manifested in testing that begins already as much as possible at the early stages of the process. In fact, the importance attributed to early identification of problems reflects a serious attitude toward risk management: A failing education system can affect the future of a country; poor-quality deliverables can affect the profitability of a company.

2.2.3 Human Perspective

Trust: The Finnish education system has trust in its students; for instance, homework is not checked. In addition, Finnish teachers trust their colleagues, principals trust their teachers, and in general, the education system is based on trust relations that encourage everyone involved in it, both students and teachers, to assume responsibility. Similarly, one way to explain the success of the agile approach is that by making the project environment transparent to all—clients and team members, management and teams, and team members and one another—this management method enhances the trust that the various interested parties have in one another. It seems that this behavior pattern ultimately leads to better results, whether it is applied in the Finnish education system or in other projects that are managed in an agile manner.

2.2.4 Agile Education and Development

Thus, several characteristics of the Finnish educational system are similar to the principles of the agile approach, and at the same time, both systems—the Finnish educational system and the agile management approach—are considered to be successful. The question raised is: Can the success of the educational system be explained by the agile approach? Or maybe it is the other way around: Maybe the success of the Finnish educational system can explain the success of agility in development processes.

In this context, it is interesting to note that in Finland, like in other Scandinavian countries, agile software development is very common. When one understands the Finnish educational system, it is easier to understand why agile work methods are so easily assimilated there.

In the spirit of the agile approach, it should be remembered that not everything is perfect in the Finnish educational system and that the education "recipe" that works so well there should not simply be copied and applied elsewhere without review and examination. In fact, the same recommendation is valid when adopting the agile approach: Organizations wishing to adopt the agile approach must adapt the practice to the place and time in which it is applied.

2.3 Summary

In this chapter, we convey the message that agile principles can be applied in any environment that wished to deliver quality, let it be an education system, research project (Tozik and Hazzan 2014), or human resources project. Thus, we establish our assertion that *Agility Anywhere* is applicable even in systems that traditionally are not conceived as projects.

References

Hazzan, O., Dubinsky, Y.: Agile Software Engineering. Springer, New York (2008)

Hazzan, O., Dubinsky, Y.: A HOT: human, organizational and technological—framework for a software engineering course. In: Proceedings of the ACM/IEEE 32nd International Conference of Software Engineering (ICSE 2010), pp. 559–566. Cape Town, South Africa

Tozik, S., Hazzan, O.: Agile research, InfoQ. http://www.infoq.com/articles/agile-academic-research?utm_campaign=infoq_content&utm_source=infoq&utm_medium=feed&utm_term=global. Accessed 14 May 2014

Chapter 3
The Agile Manifesto

Abstract This chapter introduces the main ideas that form the basis for the agile approach. Originally, the agile approach offers a professional approach for software development that encompasses human, organizational, and technological aspects of software development processes. The main ideas of agile software development processes were first introduced by the Agile Manifesto and second by presenting specific agile practices that enable agile teams to accomplish their development task on high quality. In the chapter, we present the Agile Manifesto as was published for software development and shows how it can be implemented for any projects.

Keywords Human aspects · Organizational aspects · Technological aspects · Agile manifesto · Agile practices · Quality · Agile projects · Embrace change · Customer collaboration · Interaction

3.1 The Agile Manifesto

Figure 3.1 presents the Agile Manifesto. It was formulated by seventeen software practitioners, who gathered together in February 2001 in the Wasatch Mountains of Utah, in order to find common ground for their perceptions of software development processes and to formulate what is common to what some of them have already implemented in different software organizations. The outcome of that meeting was the Agile Manifesto, which presents an alternative approach for software development processes than the approaches that had been applied during the past 40 years, from the early stages of the development of complex software systems.

The mere formulation of the Agile Manifesto implies that though there are agreed upon, common and shared principles and ideas, this common basis can be applied differently by specific development methods. Indeed, the Agile Manifesto is applied by different agile methods, such as Extreme Programming (Beck 2000) SCRUM (Schwaber 2004), Lean (Poppendieck and Poppendieck 2003), DSDM, Adaptive Software Development, Crystal, and others.

In what follows, we examine the Agile Manifesto.

O. Hazzan and Y. Dubinsky, *Agile Anywhere*, SpringerBriefs in Computer Science,
DOI 10.1007/978-3-319-10157-6_3

We are uncovering better ways of developing
software by doing it and helping others do it.
Through this work we have come to value:

Individuals and interactions over processes and tools
Working software over comprehensive documentation
Customer collaboration over contract negotiation
Responding to change over following a plan

That is, while there is value in the items on
the right, we value the items on the left more.

Fig. 3.1 Manifesto for agile software development

3.1.1 Individuals and Interactions Over Processes and Tools

This principle guides us to focus on the individuals involved in the development process rather than on the process and/or the tools. In practice, this principle guides software practitioners to give high priority to the people who participate in the development process as well as to their interaction and communication, when they develop, interact, think, discuss, and make decisions with respect to different issues related to the software development process and environment. In other words, according to this principle, one of the first considerations that should be taken into account when a decision related to the development process is made, is the influence of the decision's outcome on the people who are part of the development environment as well as on their relationships and communication.

For example, instead of investing efforts in the maintenance of a development method by using state of the art hard-to-use tools, that specify difficult-to-follow procedures that their output is useless, efforts should be channeled to the construction of a development environment that enables each of the participants (teammates, customers, management) to understand the development process, to become part of it, to contribute to it and to collaborate with all the other project stake holders.

3.1.2 Working Software Over Comprehensive Documentation

This principle delivers the message that the main target of software projects is to produce quality software products. This idea has three main implications.

First, agile software development focuses on the development itself and the creation of only these documents that are needed for the development process. Some of these essential documents, according to their characteristics and usefulness, are posted on the wall of the agile collaborative workspace so that they will be accessible to *all* the project stake holders *all the time*.

Second, agile software development processes start coding as soon as possible in order get some sense of the developed product. This early development enables the teammates and the customer to improve their understanding of the developed product and to proceed with the development process on a safer ground.

Third, from the customers' perspective, this principle advocates that customers should get a bug-less high-quality product that meets their requirements. This, of course, has direct implication on quality-related activities that agile teams perform.

As can be seen, this principle supports the first principle of the agile manifesto, by binding the people who participate in the development process with the actual development process. Such a connection inspires a culture in which software quality is one of its main values.

The importance of this principle is highlighted when its implications are compared with development processes which postpone either the beginning of the development stage (sometimes in several years) or the product quality-related activities (mainly testing). In the first case, the fact that the project production starts only after a lot of documentation has been produced, that presumably, but not in practice, captures all the customer requirements, neglects the reality that software development processes are characterized by many changes and are based on a gradual learning process. As a result, in many cases, development processes, that prepare in advance a lot of documentation without starting the actual development, do not provide eventually the customer with the needed system and in practice, inconsistencies exist between the project documentation and the actual product. In the second case, the postponement of quality-related activities leads to a situation in which the practitioners involved in the development process cannot cope successfully with the complexity of the testing activity both from cognitive and managerial perspectives.

3.1.3 Customer Collaboration Over Contract Negotiation

This principle changes the perception of the customer role in software development processes. It guides agile software development methods to base the development process on an on-going and on a daily basis contact with the customer. Such a close contact with the customers enables to cope successfully with the frequent changes that characterize software projects. This principle also points at a conception change with respect to the nature and formulation of software product contracts.

Human relationships, mainly between the customer and the management, are emphasized by this principle of the manifesto. These relations have, in turn, direct implications of the development team, which should employ specific practices to ensure these kinds of relationships and communication. These practices, when employed on a daily basis, influence directly the culture of agile organizations.

Thus, by referring to contact- and communication-related issues that aims at ensuring that the customer gets the desired product, this principle of the Agile Manifesto further supports the second principle of the agile manifesto.

3.1.4 Responding to Change Over Following a Plan

This principle guides agile software development methods to establish a development process that copes successfully with changes that are introduced during the development process, without compromising the high quality of the developed product. The rationale for this principle is derived from the recognition that customers cannot predict a priori all their requirements; therefore, a gradual process, by which the requirements are understood by the customer and are delivered to and shared with the team, should be established. Accordingly, agile software development methods inspire a process that enables to introduce changes in the developed product, that emerged based on an improved understanding of the software requirements, without necessarily increasing the cost of change introduction.

3.2 Application to Agile Projects

Based on common understandings encapsulated by the Agile Manifesto, the agile approach is applied by several basic practices that support any projects (with some modifications according to the project theme). In this section, some of these practices are introduced.

Whole team. The practice of whole team means that the project team (including all role holders and the customer) communicate in a face-to-face fashion as much as possible. It is applied in several ways.

First, the development team is colocated in a collaborative workspace—a space which supports and facilitates communication. Second, all team members participate in all the product presentations to the customer, hear the customer requirements and are active in the actual process planning. Third, role holders, that traditionally belong to separate teams (e.g., testers and designers), are integrated into the team and process.

On a daily bases, each day, during the working hours, the team is located in one space; in addition, each team member has a private space for personal tasks and professional tasks that should be carried out individually and personally. The walls of the development workspace serve as a communication means, constituting an informative and collaborative workspace. Thus, all the project stake holders can be updated at a glance at any time about the project progress and status. In addition, the entire team holds daily stand-up meetings, which usually take place in the morning. In these meetings, each team member presents in 2–3 sentences the status of his or her tasks and what he or she plans to do during the day to come, both with respect to the (development) tasks and his or her personal role.

Short releases. Agile processes are based on short releases (of about 2 months), divided into short iteration of one or 2 weeks, during which the scope of what has been decided to be delivered in the said iteration is not changed. At the end of each iteration, the deliverable is presented to the customer and the customer provides feedback to the team and sets the requirements to be delivered in the next iteration.

The detailed plan of each short iteration is carried out during a Business Day which is specifically allocated for this purpose at the beginning of each iteration. In the Business Day, all the project stake holders participate—customer, team members, users, management representatives, representative of related projects, and so on. The Business Day includes three main parts: a presentation of what was delivered in the previous iteration along with any relevant measures taken, a short reflective session in which the project process performed so far is analyzed and lessons are learnt, and the actual planning of the next iteration. At the end of the Business Day, a balanced workload is ensured among all team members.

The nature of the activities that take place during the Business Day, and the fact that a Business Day takes place every week or 2 weeks, enable all the project stake holders to construct gradually their knowledge related to the project deliverable and process, based on what they see, hear, and perform during each iteration. Specifically, during this process, the teammates improve their understanding of what should be performed, mainly due to the fact that they hear the requirements directly from the customer during the planning session.

Time estimations. In agile projects, two important practices are performed with respect to time estimation. First, the teammate, who is in charge of a specific task, also estimates the time needed for it; this practice increases the team member's responsibility and commitment to the project. Second, tasks are formulated in a way that their time estimation is possible to be set in hour resolution. This fact is important because the greater a task is, the harder it is to estimate its development time, and vice versa: the smaller the segment estimated, the more accurate its time estimation is. Consequently, the progress pace can be planned more precisely. This inspires a culture that delivers the message that plans can be set and followed in such a way that deadlines should not be postponed.

From the team perspective, since time estimations are performed at the Business Day with full team attendance, all teammates know what each team member has committed to in terms of tasks and time estimations. This fact increases the project transparency, and consequently, the teammate's responsibility to perform well. Further, the load balance, that is ensured among all team members, further reinforces trust and communication among team members.

Measures. The agile processes are accompanied with measures on which all the project stake holder decide according to their needs.

Measures enable the team to improve the process, and consequently, the deliverables. Measures also convey the message that the process should be monitored and that this monitoring should be simple, transparent, and known to all the project stakeholders.

Customer collaboration. The agile approach welcomes the customer to become part of the process. The target is to get an ongoing feedback from the customers and to move on according to their needs. This avoids the need to speculate the customers' needs, which may lead to incorrect working assumptions.

This practice implies that in agile projects all team members have access to the customer during the entire process. This direct communication channel increases both the individual interaction and the chances that the requirements are communicated correctly. Consequently, it helps the teammates to cope successfully with changes: first, there is no need to speculate the customer's needs; second, the overhead of dealing with change introduction at later stages is reduced significantly.

3.3 Summary

The Agile Manifesto established a framework, based on which a cultural (Hazzan et al. 2010) and organizational (Dubinsky et al. 2010; Talby and Dubinsky 2009) changes were introduced into the profession of software engineering. In the spirit of this book, we propose that a similar manifesto can be formulated for any theme, according to its specific characteristics and needs. Nevertheless, the spirit of the actual application of agility does not change from theme to theme.

References

Beck, K.: Extreme Programming Explained: Embrace Change. Addison-Wesley, Boston (2000)

Dubinsky, Y., Yaeli, A., Kofman, A.: Effective management of roles and responsibilities: driving accountability in software development teams. IBM Syst J **54**(2), 1–4 (2010)

Hazzan, O., Seger, T., Luria, G.: How did the creators of the agile manifesto turn from technology leaders to leaders of a cultural change? AgileQ, InfoQ, http://www.infoq.com/articles/manifesto-originators (2010). Accessed 18 Feb 2010

Poppendieck, M., Poppendieck, T.: Lean Software Development: An Agile Toolkit. Addison-Wesley Professional, Boston (2003)

Schwaber, K.: Agile Project Management with Scrum. Microsoft Press, US (2004). (Developer Best Practices)

Talby, D., Dubinsky, Y.: Governance of an agile software project. 31th International Conference of Software Engineering, ICSE, Workshop on Software Development Governance (SDG), Vancouver, Canada (2009)

Chapter 4
Change

Abstract In this chapter, we deepen the examination of the concept of change, highlighting the fact that the agile approach supports changes of different kinds. This characteristic is important since changes are an inherent element of any project and therefore should not be neglected. In order to explain how the agile approach copes with the said change, we use Plotkin's framework, borrowed from evolutionary theories, which describes how the universe copes with changes over its evolution. This exploration delivers the message that the agile approach realizes that changes are an inherent part of any process and therefore adopts several ways that support change embracement and introduction instead of blocking them. Further, in this chapter, we illustrate our Agile Guidelines by the book *Who Moved My Cheese?* (Johnson 1998), which deals with different approaches to change processes.

Keywords Change · Agile project · Plotkin's framework · Evolution · Agile process · *Who moved my cheese?*

4.1 A Conceptual Framework for Change Introduction

In his book "Darwin Machines and the Nature of Knowledge", Henry Plotkin presents the notion of change as part of the chapter that deals with the evolution of intelligence.

> Change is a universal condition of the world. If the world were unchanging, then evolution would have proceeded to some optimal point and then ceased. This has not happened. Nothing stands still, and the very occurrence of evolution is both a force for change itself and proof positive for its existence (p. 139).

The main question Plotkin poses is how we can solve the uncertainty introduced by changes. He describes two main sets of solutions to deal with the change phenomenon and explains how they enable to cope with changes (pp. 145–152).

The first set of solutions concerns with "reducing the amount of significant change," thus reducing the change scope (left branch in Fig. 4.1). One way to do it is by *reducing the period of time* (branch T in Fig. 4.1) between conception and

O. Hazzan and Y. Dubinsky, *Agile Anywhere*, SpringerBriefs in Computer Science,
DOI 10.1007/978-3-319-10157-6_4

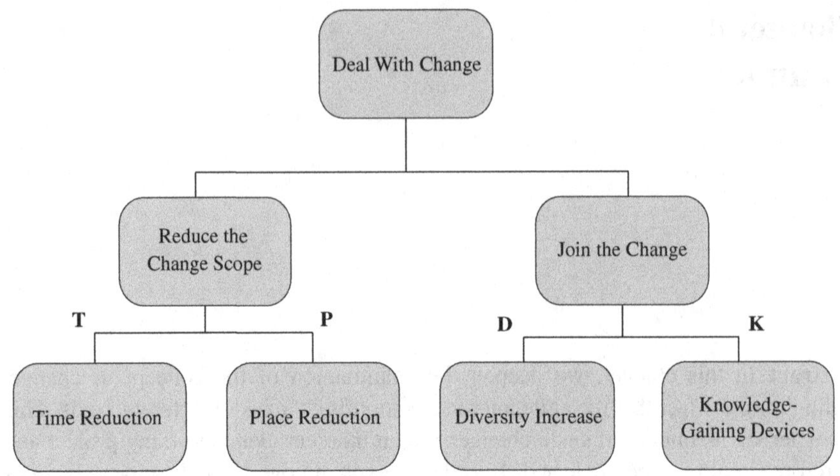

Fig. 4.1 Solutions for dealing with change (Plotkin 1997)

reproductive competence. It means keeping the ratio "life span length to numbers of offspring" low or, in other words, maintaining high reproductive output in a relatively short period of time. This way, the change is coped by keeping updated, as much as possible, the genetic instructions of each individual.

The second way to reduce the amount of significant change according to Plotkin is to *live in a relatively isolated and unpopulated place* (branch P in Fig. 4.1). A variation of this idea is parents' protection on their offspring by isolating them.

The second set of solutions for the phenomenon of change takes the form of "if you cannot beat it, join it," i.e., change the phenotypes so that they can change with and match the changing features of the world (right branch in Fig. 4.1). The first strategy to accomplish this target is to *produce large numbers of different offspring* in order to increase *diversity*. This approach increases the chances that at least some individuals will be able to cope with the change (branch D in Fig. 4.1).

The second strategy, named the "tracking option," enhances change within phenotypes by *producing phenotypes that change themselves in response to changes in the world* (branch K in Fig. 4.1). The tracking option is supported by knowledge-gaining devices which, according to Plotkin, are the immune system and the brain mechanism. The immune system operates in the sphere of *chemistry*, while the brain mechanisms, known as rationality or intelligence, operate in the sphere of the *physical world* of temporal and spatial relationships of events and objects.

4.1.1 Applying Plotkin's Framework on Changes in Requirements

Changes in the requirements are an integral part of project processes. It is usually difficult to envision how the product will look, work, function, and evolve; accordingly, customers keep changing their requirements as they improve their understanding of the features of the product they need and ask for. We can neglect this fact and block change introduction in the requirements after they have been formalized, set, and agreed upon. Alternatively, we can offer a process that allows change introduction in the requirements without reducing the product quality; this is the approach that the agile approach attempts to accomplish.

In what follows we present several agile ideas within Plotkin's framework.

Reducing the change scope—time reduction mechanism
Customer has an opportunity to update the requirements at the end of each *short releases and iteration*; clearly, this is a mechanism for time reduction.

Analysis shows that cost of change introduction in this fashion remains constant. This is because it allows updating the requirements on a small scale as soon as it is realized that a different feature is needed than the one that has been envisioned in an earlier stage. Under this working assumption, customers are not forced to present a full requirement list and do not need to assume what will probably be needed, and therefore, in the planning sessions, they ask only for relevant requirements. Thus, at the end of an agile project, only features that the customer needs are produced.

Reducing the change scope—space reduction mechanism
Space is reduced by the colocation of the team and the customer in the workspace. This space includes also the walls that serve as a communicative means, so that all the relevant information is accessible to all.

Join the change—diversity mechanism
The discussion about diversity is of high relevance in this context of change in requirements. This is because diversity welcomes new ideas and perspectives that are so predominant in change introduction processes.

Join the change—mechanism of knowledge gaining devices
The agile approach applies several practices that can be characterized as knowledge-gaining devices. Among them, we mention the customer and reflections and retrospectives processes.

4.2 Illustrations from *Who Moved My Cheese*?

The book *Who Moved My Cheese? An Amazing Way to Deal with Change in Your Work and in Your Life* (Johnson 1998) describes different approaches toward change and toward the realization of the need for change. It teaches us how to deal with change, that different people approach change differently, and that a specific mind-set should be adopted when one gets into a Change process. The book tells the story of two mice and two "little people," who had to leave their comfort zone and to find a new resource for their cheese after it had been stopped supplied.

In what follows we present several illustrative quotes for each of the three agile anywhere categories—characteristics, behavior, and emotion. The message is clear: Agility, as a way to approach change as well as the change process itself, is relevant anywhere. We note that the book was published more or less when the agile approach started being implemented in software development processes. Not surprisingly, the following quotes use common terms from the agile world, such as "embrace change" and "simplicity." We recommend reading the book, and specifically, the summary of all the lessons learned from the story (e.g., Monitor Change and Adapt To Change Quickly, p. 74), and see their resemblances to the agile principles.

4.2.1 Change Characteristics

The following quotes deliver the idea that change happens all the time, and therefore, one should expect change, be ready to change all the time, and take a proactive approach:

- P. 18: Everyone knows that not all change is good or even necessary. But in a world that is constantly changing, it is to our advantage to learn how to adapt and enjoy something better.
- P. 45: Haw said, "Sometimes, Hem, things change and they are never the same again. This looks like one of those times. That's life! Live moves on. And so should we."
- P. 63: Now he [Haw] realized it was natural for change to continually occur, whether you expect it or not.

Simplicity—one of the basic ideas of agility—is also mentioned in the book as a characteristic of a change process:

- P. 17: In *The Story* you will see that the two mice do better when they are faced with change because they keep things simple, while the two little people's complex brains and human emotions complicate things.
- P. 71: He knew he had learned something useful about moving on from his mice friends, Sniff and Scurry. They kept life simple. They didn't overanalyze or overcomplicate things. When the situation changed and the Cheeses had been moved, they changes and moved with the Cheeses.

4.2.2 Behavior While Change

Taking responsibility:

- P. 50: Whenever he started to get discouraged, he reminded himself that what he was doing, as uncomfortable as it was at the moment, was in reality much better than staying in the Cheeseless situation. He was taking control, rather than simply letting things happen to him.
  Then he reminded himself, if Sniff and Scurry could move on, so could he!
  P. 75: While Haw still had a great supply of cheese, he often went out into the Maze and explored new areas to stay in touch with what was happening around him. He knew it was safer to be aware of his real choices than to isolate himself in his comfort zone.

Embrace change:

- P. 65: He [Haw] knew that when you change what you believe, you change what you do.
  You can believe that a change will harm you and resist it. Or you can believe that finding New Cheeses will help you and embrace the change.

Reflection:

- P. 70: As Haw enjoyed the New Cheese, he reflected on what he had learned.
  He realized that when he had been afraid to change he had been holding on to the illusion of Old Cheese that was no longer there.
- P. 71: He [Haw] reflected on the mistakes he had made in the past and used them to plan for the future. He knew that you could learn to deal with change.
  You could be more aware of the need to keep things simple, be flexible, and move quickly.

4.2.3 Change Emotions

Resistance to change:

- P. 41: "I'm getting too old for that," Hem said. "And I'm afraid I'm not interested in getting lost and making a fool of myself. Are you?"
- P. 51: Mold may even have begun to grow on the Old Cheese, although he [Haw] hadn't noticed it. He had to admit however, that if he had wanted to, he probably could have seen what was coming. But he didn't.

Uncertainty:

- P. 40: He [Haw] believed they [the mice—Sniff and Scurry] might be having a hard time, as running through the Maze usually involved some uncertainty. But he also knew that it was likely to only last for a while.

Fear and Courage:

- P. 44: He [Haw] painted a picture in his mind. He saw himself venturing out into the Maze with a smile on his face.
  While this picture surprised him, it made him feel god. He saw himself getting lost now and then in the Maze, but felt confident he would eventually find New Cheese out there and all the good things that came with it. He gathered his courage.
- P. 49: He [Haw] knew sometimes some fear can be good. When you are afraid things are going to get worse if you don't do something. It can prompt you into action. But it is not good when you are so afraid that it keeps you from doing anything.
  He looked at his right, to the part of the Maze where he had never been, and felt the fear.
  Then, he took a deep breath, turned right into the Maze, and jogged slowly, into the unknown.

4.3 Summary

In this chapter, we present two instances in which agile ideas are applied—evolution and a story that aims to deliver the notion of coping with change. We choose these examples, among many others we are familiar with, to illustrate the vast variety of cases in which these ideas were found to be valuable and thus to further support our choice in the title of the book *Agile Anywhere.*

References

Johnson, S.: Who Moved My Cheese? An Amazing Way to Deal with Change in Your Work and in Your Life. Putnam Adult, New York City (1998)

Plotkin, H.: Darwin Machines and the Nature of Knowledge. Harvard University Press, Cambridge (1997)

Chapter 5
Team

Abstract This chapter focuses on teams and leadership—both are most influential factors of projects' success. Consequently, agility highly appreciates and supports them. One agile practice which is highlighted in this chapter is applying a role scheme which fosters the interconnections and dependencies between the members of agile teams and enhances creativity, responsibility, accountability, diversity, and measure collection. The role scheme delivers the message that each team member can contribute to the project also on the team level, beyond his or her individual contribution, and that the mutual contribution of the individuals in the team creates a whole which is greater than the sum of its parts. Another agile practice which this chapter deals with is leadership that is the ability to influence people, leading them to behave in a certain way in order to achieve the group's goals. Leadership is independent of job titles and descriptions. However, leaders usually need the power derived from their organizational position in order to lead. The agile approach suggests a leadership style that emphasizes the team spirit and empowers the team members to be highly committed to the project.

Keywords Agile teams · Leadership · Projects' success · Role scheme · Creativity · Responsibility · Accountability · Diversity · Measures · Mutual contribution · The whole is greater than the sum of its parts · Group's goals · Organizational position · Leadership style · Team spirit · Team member commitment

5.1 A Role Scheme of Agile Teams

Project teams are needed for the accomplishment of the project deliverables. Usually, this cannot be accomplished by one person, and teamwork is needed.

According to (Humphrey 2000), a team consists of at least two people who are working toward a common goal/objective/mission, where each person has been assigned a specific role to perform and where a completion of the mission requires some form of dependency among team members (p. 19). The assignment of roles

O. Hazzan and Y. Dubinsky, *Agile Anywhere*, SpringerBriefs in Computer Science,
DOI 10.1007/978-3-319-10157-6_5

serves as a means for splitting, among all the team members, the responsibility for the project management and progress. When the responsibility is split among all teammates, each aspect of the project is treated by one teammate and each teammate feels a responsibility for the said specific aspect. Both the projects as a whole and each of the individual team members are benefited from this kind of organization.

For illustration, we present a possible role scheme in an agile software development team (Table 5.1). The role scheme consists of four groups of roles which expands and integrates the role schemes suggested by different agile methods (Dubinsky and Hazzan 2004, 2006).

As can be seen, in the case of a software project, the different roles address different aspects of the development process; this point of view can be applied to any agile project.

Table 5.1 Illustration—roles in an Agile software team

Group of roles	Role	Description
Leading group	Coach	Coordinates and solves group problems, leads and guides development sessions
	Tracker	Measures the group progress by measures defined by the team, the customer, and the organization, manages the workspace boards, manages the team diary/collective memory
	Methodologist	Guides the team with respect to the working methodology, inspires its spirit, answers questions, looks for solutions to problems, etc
Customer group	Proxy-user	Holds a user centric approach, e.g., performs an on-going user evaluation of the product
	Proxy-customer	Holds a customer-oriented approach, e.g., tells customer stories, provides feedback, and defines acceptance tests
	Acceptance tester	Defines tests with the customer and develops acceptance tests
Code group	Designer	Maintains current design, works to simplify design, and promotes refactoring activities
	Unit tester	Guides a test-driven development process, e.g., establishes an automated test suite, guides and supports others in the development of unit tests
	Continuous integrator	Establishes the integration environment, publishes and guides rules pertaining to the addition of new code
	Code reviewer	Maintains source control, establishes and refines coding standards
Maintenance group	Presenter	Plans and organizes iteration/release presentations, e.g., demos and measures
	Documenter	Plans and organizes the project documentation: process documentation, user's guide, and installation instructions
	Installer	Plans and ensures the assimilation process

5.1.1 Human Perspective on the Role Scheme

Social Aspect

- A personal role increases teammates' involvement, communication, accountability, responsibility, and commitment to the process and to their team.
- Team members wish to have a specific role in addition to their tasks in order to increase their influence and involvement in the project management.

Cognitive Aspect

- Since each team member approaches the project from one specific perspective, each team member can focus on this one specific aspect without being distracted by the multifaceted nature of the process. Consequently, each team member gradually improves his or her understanding about the said aspect.
- The role scheme supports team members' thinking in terms of different levels of abstraction. On the one hand, each team member sees his or her task on a relatively low level of abstraction; on the other hand, the personal role of each team member enables each of them to gain a global overview of the project on a higher level of abstraction.
- The role scheme enhances knowledge distribution since each team member specializes in one domain and shares his or her knowledge with the other team members. In addition, since the role scheme leads to knowledge distribution, no harm happens when one team member leaves the team. In this case, the other team members have a reasonable amount of knowledge to continue with respect to the said role.
- The role scheme supports the individual's professional development. Team members perform their roles and improve the role performance while learning the practice that their role represents. In turn, they became experts in the specific aspect of the project on which their personal role focuses. In addition, when a team member feels that he or she has exploited the role contribution to his or her professional development and wishes to hold another role in the team, role rotation can take place.

5.1.2 Using the Role Scheme to Scale Agile Projects

The role scheme supports also the scaling up of agile projects. Suppose, we have five agile teams as part of one project, each of them applies the role scheme. In this setting, weekly role meetings are set for each role, in which all the role holders from all the teams participate. For example, in a system project, a weekly meeting of all testers of the project takes place; a bi-weekly meeting of all the integrators takes place, etc. It is recommended that these role meetings are scheduled at the same time in order not to collide with the working sessions of the teams. In these meetings, project-wide issues are discussed, to allow the project management proceeds in one direction.

The use of the role scheme for scaling up purposes enhances also knowledge distribution. On the individual level, each team members has the opportunity to communicate with other practitioners, beyond his or her team, to present the knowledge his or him team gained so far with respect to the said role and to serve as a bridge between the team and the organization with respect to the aspect of the project of which she or he is in charge. On the team level, each team may benefit also from the wisdom and experiences gained by other teams. For example, the team representatives may bring into the role meetings a problem with which their team faces, and ask the other role representatives whether their experience can contribute to the problem solution. Such a dialogue creates a knowledge infrastructure for the entire project from which all teams can benefit. On the organization level, and based on the individual and team levels, knowledge is distributed, managed, and maintained.

5.2 Leadership

Leadership is a social phenomenon required for achieving group's goals (Nirenberg 2002). The agile approach adopts a leadership style that empowers the people involved in the project. For example, instead of promoting the idea that "Leaders should keep the power to themselves in order not to loose it," the agile approach fosters the idea that "Leaders gains power from its sharing." This idea is expressed, among other ways, by the transparency of the agile process that makes information accessible to anyone and enables each team member to be accountable and fully involved in the project.

Table 5.2 (adopted from Huff and Moeslein 2005; originally from Drath 1998) presents the evolution of leadership models, indicating a shift in leadership perception.

In agile projects, "Leadership is generally taken to mean the ability to influence others in a group to act in a particular way to achieve group goals" (Hughes and Cotterell 2002, p. 222). In terms of Table 5.2, the agile approach fits the "modern" and "future" leadership styles, on which we elaborate in what follows.

With respect to the Idea of Leadership, the notion of Common Goals in agile teams is mainly expressed by customer on going collaboration along the entire process and by the information transparency, which enables each team member

Table 5.2 Evolving models of leadership (Drath, 1998: 408)

	Ancient	Traditional	Modern	Future
Idea of leadership	Domination	Influence	Common goals	Reciprocal relations
Action of leadership	Commanding followers	Motivating followers	Creating inner commitment	Mutual meaning making
Focus of the leadership development	Power of the leader	Interpersonal skills of the leader	Self-knowledge of the leader	Interactions within the group

know what these common goals are and participate in the planning and presentation meetings related to these goals. Reciprocal relations relate to high levels of cooperation, confidence, and trust among team members. In (Hazzan and Dubinsky, 2005), we use game theory to explain reciprocation in development environments by employing the prisoners' dilemma.

With respect to the Action of Leadership (Table 5.2), the role scheme creates and enhances inner commitment since each team member has an additional specific role that assists the project leadership (Dubinsky and Hazzan 2006). Though team members are committed, mutual meaning is still needed to provide a relevant and meaningful product.

The focus of leadership development aspect in Table 5.2 shows how the leader position should be developed to improve leadership. While the three first columns focus on the leader, the "future" column deals with the group and its interactions. As the level of leadership increases, the group interactions lead the team, i.e., the way team members communicate, reflect, and collaborate enables the team to lead itself as if there is no leader, while, in practice, high-quality leadership exists.

5.3 Summary

This chapter introduces the concept of role assignment to team members, which, on the personal level improves their understanding of the project and its deliveries, and on the team level, improves the process and quality. In addition, we discuss leadership in agile environments and posed in within a framework of evolution of leadership models.

References

Drath, W.H.: Approaching the future of leadership development. In: McCauley, C.D., Moxley, R.S., Van Velsor, E. (eds.) The Center for Creative Leadership: Handbook of Leadership Development 403–432 San Francisco. Jossey-Bass, CA (1998)

Dubinsky, Y., Hazzan, O.: Roles in agile software development teams. In: 5th International Conference on Extreme Programming and Agile Processes in Software Engineering, Garmisch-Partenkirchen, Germany, pp. 157–165 (2004)

Dubinsky, Y., Hazzan, O.: Using a role scheme to derive software project quality. J. Syst. Architect. **52**(11), 693–699 (2006)

Hazzan, O., Dubinsky, Y.: Cognitive and social perspectives of software development methods: The case of Extreme Programming. In: Proceedings of the 6th International Conference on Extreme Programming and Agile Processes in Software Engineering, pp. 74–81 (2005)

Huff, A.S., Moeslein, K.: An agenda for understanding individual leadership in corporate leadership systems. In: Cooper, C.L. (eds.) Leadership and Management in the 21st Century: Business Challenges of the Future, pp. 248–270. Oxford University Press Inc., New York (2005)

Hughes, B., Cotterell, M.: Software Project Management, 3rd edn. McGraw-Hill, New York (2002)

Humphrey, W.: Introduction to the Team Software Process. Addison-Wesley, MA (2000)

Nirenberg, J.: Global leadership. Capstone Wiley (2002)

Chapter 6
Customers and Users

Abstract The agile manifesto emphasizes "individuals and interactions." When practitioners are asked who are these individuals, most of them would probably mention different roles like system analysts, developers, and testers. The agile approach increases the awareness to additional essential roles in the project, like the customer, who is one of the most important project stakeholders. The users, at the same time, are somehow wrongly neglected, since a common misconception is that the customer represents all users. In this chapter, these two roles are distinguished and described by addressing their main responsibilities.

Keywords Users · User evaluation · Customer · Information sharing · Transparency · Collaboration · Human–computer interaction (HCI) · Reflective session · Feedback

6.1 The Customer

6.1.1 Agile Practices Related to the Customer Role

The customer's position and role is one of the main changes that the agile approach introduced into processes in general and into team members' conception of the customer role in particular. This customer position in agile environments is central. It is based on ongoing communication between the customer and the team members, both with respect to the project requirements, as well as with respect to the way testing is performed, and how the suitability of the deliverables to the user's needs is achieved. This communication is established with the aid of several practices. In this chapter, we focus on the practice of planning and how it fosters customer–teammates communication and bridge the gap (if exists) between the customer's and the teammates' worldviews. As it turns out, the customer role is not only supported by several practices, but rather it also fosters agile characteristics, such as information sharing and transparency. The main

O. Hazzan and Y. Dubinsky, *Agile Anywhere*, SpringerBriefs in Computer Science,
DOI 10.1007/978-3-319-10157-6_6

idea delivered is that the agile approach supports the customer role and enables the required collaboration needed for the production of high-quality products.

The conception of the customer role in agile environments is significantly extended. This new meaning is not limited to listening to the customer; rather, it also implies that the customer decisions are followed. This conception can be implemented since the customer presents on-site and is involved in the process continuously, as is presented in what follows.

6.1.2 Project Schedule and the Business Day

A project schedule comprises of short releases of three to four months. Each release includes short iterations of one to few weeks. As part of a release planning, the following activities take place.

- The customer describes the project vision, the project main stories, and the guidelines according to which priorities will be set.
- The team members present their vision about the project deliverables.
- The project manager presents his or her view of the process as well as his or her personal expectations.
- Other stake holders present their expectations from the project.

This part of a release planning takes place after the presentation of the previous release has completed, and a retrospective session between the two releases has been facilitated.

A *Business Day* (Dubinsky et al. 2005a) takes place between each two consequent iterations of the release. The rest of the iteration days are working days. In the Business Day, in addition to the team and the customer, other project stake holders are invited to participate, including managers and external parties, such as customer associates and users.

In the first part of the Business Day, the previous iteration is summarized. In the second part, after a reflective session takes place, the next iteration planning starts. The Business Day between iterations is time-boxed up to one working day, and the exact schedule of the different activities may vary between projects. During the Business Day, the customer has a significant role, as is explained in what follows.

The **presentation of the accomplishments of the ending iteration** demonstrates the main new features. In the case of a software project, the presented features are associated with specific customer stories of the ending iteration, when a customer story is defined in (Beck and Fowler 2000) as follows: "The story is the unit of functionality in [a] … project. We demonstrate progress by delivering tested, integrated code that implements a story. A story should be understandable to customers and developers, testable, valuable to the customer, and small enough so that programmers can build half a dozen in an iteration (p. 45)." The customer business interest is also emphasized: "The most important stories to do first are the ones that contain the highest business value. Beware of sequencing stories based on technical dependencies. Most of the time, the dependencies are less important than the value (p. 63)."

During the presentation, each team member presents his or her work. This activity raises team members' accountability for at least two reasons. First, they should present a high-quality deliverable that answers a specific customer story. Second, they should present this output every iteration in front of all project stakeholders, including managers and external parties, as well as their own team. Furthermore, since each team member shares the information with all the other people involved and answers their questions, the overall understanding of the project components and features increases.

The **measures review** includes a presentation and analysis of the ending iteration's metrics. In the case of software development projects, the following four metrics are interesting for many agile teams (Dubinsky et al. 2005b): The product metric (amount of written and passed tests), the pulse metric (a measure of continuous integration; Beck 2000), the burn-down metric (an estimation of the convergence of the release/iteration goals), and fault metrics (number of new and open defects).

The goal of this element of the iteration summary is twofold. First is to present the data to the entire team in order to base the individuals' perception (for example, about product quality, time lost to overhead, etc.) on facts. Second is to openly discuss the reasons behind the metrics, and how, if needed, the process can be improved.

The customer role in this part is "to be there," to increase process and progress transparency, and to be updated continuously about the project status. The decisions taken by the customer are also influenced by the information provided in the measures presentation. For example, if the measures indicate that a specific component is more complex then it seemed when planned, the customer can decide to change the development scope and/or the priorities. The customer can also add measures of his or her own interest. This way the teammates improve their understanding with respect to the customer emphases and priorities.

The **customer feedback** is a short, informal verbal summary of the iteration, given by the customer. This direct feedback usually focuses on the product rather than on the process. It is important to include the customer's message in the iteration summary to signal the customer's importance in the process. It also helps in focusing people's attention on the product as an end goal, rather than their own specific tasks.

The **reflective session**'s goal is to discuss a specific issue in the process, and to change the process if needed. This part of the Business Day, whose topic is announced before it takes place, is considered as a timeout to stop considering the regular, mainly technical, issues and to think about other kind of topics. Usually, people enjoy this timeout, cooperate in bringing new issues to the discussion and volunteer to take the responsibility to follow up things that they find interesting and relevant for them.

The **Planning the next iteration** starts immediately after the previous iteration is summarized and its reflective sessions ends. As in the first part of the Business Day, the customer and all team members participate; other people who have interest in the project are invited.

First, the customer tells the stories that were prepared in advance to be developed in the next iteration. To the customer list, stories from other sources are added, such as: incomplete stories from previous iterations, refactoring tasks, and user interface stories that emerged from the user evaluation. The customer role in this part is to prioritize the stories so that all the people involved, including all team members, hear and realize the customer's perspective with respect to the story importance.

Second, based on earlier work, the top-prioritized tasks are described and estimated by the team members who take ownership on them. The actual planning is set according to the available time of the team members in the coming iteration.

Finally, the workloads between the team members are balanced.

The iteration planning is shaped differently according to project goals; nevertheless, it is important to follow the following guidelines:

- Time is an important resource and should be managed wisely.
- The smaller a task is, the more accurate its time estimation is; Thus, product delivery on time and of high quality is better ensured.
- An ordered professional work environment is appreciated and desired by professional practitioners; chaos frustrates professional practitioners, especially because in chaotic situations, products are of low quality and their professionalism is doubted.
- Fairness and a cooperative work environment are valued by professional practitioners; an open and transparent work distribution, in which all parties are involved, increases practitioners' security, trust, and cooperation.

6.2 The User

6.2.1 Agile and HCI Practices Related to the User

While the customer is one or few people who either actually pays or has other kinds of interest in the process, in the context of most projects, the user is, in fact, the main client. This is where the agile paradigm meets the world of human–computer interaction (HCI). HCI adds the user perspective by offering user evaluation methods that provide indicators for the usability and functionality of the project deliverables (Dix et al. 2004; Norman 2006). The main idea delivered is the mutual connections and contributions between agile concepts and HCI practices. Specifically, on one hand, the user evaluation is fostered by the agile process; on the other hand, the product benefits from keeping its internals updated according to the ongoing user evaluation.

The human–computer interaction (HCI) field has emerged at the early 1960s. It deals with the interface design and evaluation and with the interactions between users and systems. The main goal of the HCI field is to improve these interfaces and interactions according to users' needs. This is done by rigorous techniques that involve users and HCI design experts in the design of the user interface and evaluation process. Norman (2006) suggests abandoning the traditional HCI approach of "study first, design second" and to try the "design, then study" approach. This suggestion is influenced by the agile approach.

Since usability is "The extent to which a product can be used by specified users to achieve specified goals with effectiveness, efficiency and satisfaction in a specified context of use." (ISO 9241-11 1998), it is essential to integrate the users in the project process. This importance is highlighted when the most useful indicators in measuring the usability level of a product, as is defined by the ISO 9241 standards, are examined:

- Effectiveness in use, which encompasses accuracy and completeness through which users achieve certain results.
- Efficiency in use, which addresses resources utilized in relation to accuracy and completeness.
- Satisfaction in use, which includes freedom from inconveniences and positive attitude toward the use of a product.

6.2.2 User Centered Design (UCD)

The integration of the user in the project environment is accomplished by the user-centered design (UCD) approach, which is a set of design techniques that emphasize the user needs during the design of the user interface. The outcome of the user interface design phase should support usability of the interfaces and interactions. This is achieved by user evaluation by evaluation techniques (Rogers et al. 2002; Vredenburg et al. 2002).

Evaluation of user interfaces aims at assessing the extent of system functionality while the user interacts with and gains experience with the system, as well as identifies specific problems related to the system (Dix et al. 2004). There are two main types of evaluation: expert-based evaluation and user-based evaluation.

In **expert-based evaluation**, a designer or an HCI expert assesses the design of the user interfaces based on known cognitive principles or empirical results. The **user-based evaluation** is based on user participation, i.e., evaluation that involves the people who are going to use the system. User-based evaluation techniques include: observations, questionnaires, interviews, and physiological monitoring methods. User-based evaluation can be conducted in a laboratory and/or in the field.

Surprisingly, it is known that the best evaluation results come from small groups with no more than five users, conducted in several iterations (Nielsen and Landauer 1993). Therefore, an evaluation process is not an expensive process as can be wrongly conceived. For example, (Nielsen and Landauer 1993) describe iterative design in which the evaluation of five users reveals 85 % of the usability problems. Accordingly, the design of the user interface has been changed and has been re-evaluated to check if problems have been fixed and if new problems have not emerged. Indeed, re-evaluation iterations probe deeper usability problems.

When combining UCD with agile approach, we observe that they mutually benefit each other (Blomkvist 2005; Humayoun et al. 2009, 2011); hence, users should be constantly involved in the process. Accordingly, in agile projects, users are constantly involved in the process and their role is highlighted by the agile approach. The user evaluation contributes to the set of measures used for the steering and directing of the projects as well as enhances the design of user interfaces, which are part of the project.

6.3 Summary

In this chapter, the customers' and users' roles in agile projects are described. The activities, by which the customer navigates the project process by telling the stories, prioritizing stories, and giving ongoing feedback to the teammates with respect to the evolved artifacts, are laid out. This kind of collaboration sets the atmosphere needed for dealing with change requests, thus establishing a process that leads to high-quality product (also) from the customer perspective.

User involvement in agile projects is also discussed to deliver the needed user interface. For this purpose, a user-centered approach is adopted and goes hand in hand with the agile approach.

References

Beck, K.: Extreme Programming Explained: Embrace Change. Addison-Wesley, Boston (2000)

Beck, K., Fowler, M.: Planning Extreme Programming. Addison-Wesley, Boston (2000)

Blomkvist, S.: Towards a model for bridging agile development and user-centered design. In: Seffah, A., Gulliksen, J., Desmarais, M. (eds.) Human-Centered Software Engineering—Integrating Usability in The Development Process. Springer, Dordrecht, The Netherlands (2005). (Published as a book chapter)

Dix, A., Finlay, J., Abowd, G.D., Beale, R.: Human-Computer-Interaction, 3rd edn. Scotprint, Haddington (2004)

Dubinsky, Y., Hazzan, O., Keren, A.: Introducing extreme programming into a software project at the Israeli Air Force. In: Proceedings of the 6th International Conference on Extreme Programming and Agile Processes in Software Engineering, Sheffield University, UK (2005a)

Dubinsky, Y., Talby. D., Hazzan, O., Keren, A.: Agile metrics at the israeli air force. In: Agile Conference, Denver, Colorado (2005b)

Humayoun, S., Dubinsky, Y., Catarci, T.: UEMan: a tool to manage user evaluation in development environments. In: 31th International Conference Software Engineering, ICSE, Vancouver, Canada (2009)

Humayoun, S.R., Dubinsky, Y., Catarci, T.: A Three-Fold Integration Framework to Incorporate User-Centered Design into Agile Software Development. In: Human Centered Design, HCII 2011, pp. 55–64. Springer, Heidelberg (2011)

ISO 9241-11: Ergonomic Requirements for Office Work with Visual Display Terminals: Guidance on Usability (1998)

Nielsen, J., Landauer, T.K.: A mathematical model of the finding of usability problems. In: Proceedings of ACM INTERCHI'93 Conference, pp. 206–213. Amsterdam, The Netherlands (1993)

Norman, D.: Why doing user observations first is wrong. ACM Interactions, July–August (2006)

Rogers, Y., Preece, J., Sharp, H.: Interaction Design: Beyond Human-Computer Interaction. Wiley, New York (2002)

Vredenburg, K., Isensee, S., Righi, C.: User-Centered Design: An Integrated Approach. Software Quality Institute Series, Prentice Hall PTR (2002)

Chapter 7
Time

Abstract Time is addressed differently by different people and cultures; for example, in western culture, time is sometimes associated with financial profit, i.e., "Time is money." Time plays a special role in agile projects: The project schedule should be met, the product should be delivered on time, and teammates estimate the time they need to complete their tasks. Furthermore, time is boxed for each activity, and when needed, instead of "moving" deadlines, the scope is changed according to the customer priorities. This conception is supported by agility in different ways that not only enable to work in a sustainable pace, but also result in high-quality products. This chapter examines how time issues are expressed in agile environments. It addresses three ways by which time is managed effectively by agile methods—sustainable pace, time measurements, and prioritizing tasks—and time-related problems associated with software projects.

Keywords Time · Cultures · Role in agile projects · Project schedule · Time estimation · Time box · Scope · Sustainable pace · Time management · Time measurements · Task prioritization

7.1 Sustainable Pace

Sustainable pace means that an agile process is carried out in a reasonable number of hours, which are well planned and enable to be productive and produce quality products (Reifer 2002).

This idea is manifested also in Finnish educational system, which is considered as one of the best education systems in the world. Specifically, even though children in Finland spend fewer hours at school than do children in many other Western countries, they achieve better results. These results are apparently attained by utilizing the school hours in a way that encourages significant learning processes. Indeed, it is apparent that in Finland, students are active, improve their skills, and teach each other in classes of 15 students and two teachers.

O. Hazzan and Y. Dubinsky, *Agile Anywhere*, SpringerBriefs in Computer Science,
DOI 10.1007/978-3-319-10157-6_7

This phenomenon is also expressed in agile software development. Efficient time management in agile environments supports the production of high-quality product in a limited, relatively smaller number of hours per day, as opposed to the practice of working long hours under other management methods.

7.2 Time Measurements

One of the common measures of agile projects is the estimated time for tasks-to-be-performed versus the actual time to accomplish them. In order to control the project progress, this kind of measure can be inspected on a daily basis, weekly basis or monthly basis, according to the agile project.

For example, in the case of agile software projects, the white boards of the collaborative workspace constantly present a graph that its horizontal axis represents the iteration days and its vertical axes indicate number of hours. Each day, the tracker adds two new points to a graph that represent the project progress. The first one—the "total expected" point—represents the cumulative estimations of all *completed* tasks until the previous day; the second point—the "total done" point—represents the cumulative actual time devoted to those tasks. A completed task is counted only when the developer in charge completes its coding, unit testing, and integration into the developed system.

7.3 Prioritizing Tasks

Covey's concept of *First Things First* (Covey et al. 1994) introduces an organizing framework that may explain how agile processes guide agile teams to focus on what is *important* rather than on what is urgent.

Covey suggests dividing the activities on which a person works to four quadrants (see Table 7.1). The idea is to direct practitioners to focus on Quadrant II, which contains items that are non-urgent but important. As it turns out, these items are the ones we are more likely to neglect but should focus on in order to achieve effectiveness and quality. In the context of software development, this phenomenon can be explained by the fact that people tend to be distracted from what is important because it is sometimes difficult to focus on the development of an intangible product, such as software.

Agile software development guides practitioners to implement activities from the second quadrant—the *quality quadrant* (important and not urgent), inspiring a

Table 7.1 Time management—importance versus urgency

I. Urgent and important	II. Not urgent and important
III. Urgent and not important	IV. Not urgent and not important

Table 7.2 A sample of practitioners' suggestions for each quadrant

I. *Urgent and important*	II. *Not urgent and important*
Production problems Fixing bugs that prevent progress Preparing a presentation after it has been postponed till the last minute	Iteration planning Design Learning new technologies Refactoring Tracking—follow-up and control Testing Taking care of infrastructure Preparing a presentation on time
III. *Urgent and not important* Working on management assignments that arrive late and have tight deadlines Helping other team members with urgent tasks that are not important for me	IV. *Not urgent and not important* Mingling Personal arrangements/errands

work process that is composed of important (and not urgent) activities and eliminating the performance of urgent activities (whether important or not) during the course of the project. Table 7.2 presents a sample of activities suggested by team members for each quadrant. As can be seen, Quadrant II—the quality quadrant—contains agile activities and practices. The project manager noted that: "*The second quadrant is characterized by teamwork—because of the team, I do what is important and I do not give up*."

7.4 Time-Related Problems of Software Projects

We illustrate the importance of time in agile software projects, by quoting Brooks' classic book *The Mythical Man-Month* (Brooks 1975, 1995):

> "More software projects have gone awry for lack of calendar time than for all other causes combined. Why is this cause a disaster so common?
>
> First, our techniques of estimating are poorly developed. More seriously, they reflect an unvoiced assumption which is quite untrue, i.e., that all will go well.
>
> Second, our estimating techniques fallaciously confuse effort with progress, hiding the assumption that man and months are interchangeable.
>
> […]
>
> Fifth, when schedule slippage is recognized, the natural (and traditional) response is to add manpower. Like dousing a fire with gasoline, this makes matter worse, much worse. More fire requires more gasoline, and thus begins a regenerative cycle which ends in disaster." (p. 14)

In software engineering, time plays a special role and it is one of the most important factors, dominating software development processes. One reason that makes time so crucial in software development is that software development does not progress linearly. This fact is expressed by Brooks' statement that, in software projects, months and people are not interchangeable (Brooks 1975, 1995). Hazzan and Dubinsky (2007) outline time-related problems of software projects, such as: Bottlenecks, project planning and schedule, time estimation, time pressure, and late delivery, to illustrate the significant role of time management in agile software development processes, as described above.

7.5 Summary

This chapter discusses the concepts of time and time management in agile environments. It reflects the tight approach of the agile approach to time, which ensures a controlled process that enables to increase product quality.

References

Brooks, F.P.: The Mythical Man-Month—Essays on Software Engineering. Addison-Wesley, Boston (1975, 1995)

Covey, S., Merrill, A.R., Merrill, R.R.: First Things First. Free Press (1994)

Hazzan, O., Dubinsky, Y.: The software engineering timeline: a time management perspective. In: Proceedings of the IEEE International Conference on Software—Science, Technology and Engineering, pp. 95–103. Herzelia, Israel (2007)

Reifer, D.J.: How to get the most out of XP/Agile methods. In: Proceedings of the Second XP universe and First Agile Universe Conference, pp. 185–196. Chicago, IL (2002)

Chapter 8
Measures

Abstract There is a consensus that the performance, control and management of every process and activity can be improved using measures to monitor them. The agile approach promotes a constant tracking during the entire project. Further, the tracker role includes the responsibility to define and refine the measures, data collection, and measure presentation. Some measures are presented daily, like the daily progress within the iteration; some measures are presented each iteration, like the iteration progress within the release; yet, other measures are presented every release, like customer level of satisfaction or product testability. When measures are addressed on a regular basis, all teammates and stakeholders can view them, give feedback, and suggest measure refinements. Thus, their understanding of the project is improved, their accountability for the project deliverables is fostered, project transparency is increased, and cognitive complexity is reduced. We answer the following questions as they are expressed in agile projects: (1) Why are measures needed? (2) Who decides what is measured? (3) What should be measured? (4) When are measures taken? (5) How are measures taken? (6) Who does take measure? (7) How are measures used?

Keywords Measures · Tracking · The tracker role · Data collection · Measure refinements · Accountability

8.1 Why Are Measures Needed?

Measures are used in order to control and monitor project processes and the evolvement of its deliverables. A set of measures, defined for a specific project, should adhere to the following characteristics:

- The measures should be mapped to the project goals. It is recommended that this mapping is regularly assessed in order first, to ensure that no redundant measures are taken and second, to check the compliance of the different goals based on the existing measures (Dubinsky et al. 2008).
- The measure collection should not affect the process progress that the measures control.

O. Hazzan and Y. Dubinsky, *Agile Anywhere*, SpringerBriefs in Computer Science,
DOI 10.1007/978-3-319-10157-6_8

In the case of a specific project, for example, a goal might be to shorten delivery time; consequently, among different subgoals related to this goal, the project progress can be monitored on a daily basis. This measure is then can be viewed on a daily basis, an iteration basis, and a release basis.

Measurements enable an agile team to get constant feedback from the different components of the project: people and deliverables. A measure that is people-oriented can be customer satisfaction or the amount of team overtime hours (for the sustainable pace measure). A measure that is deliverable-oriented can be functional coverage, which shows the degree to which the deliverables fulfill the project functional requirements. The ongoing presentation of the measures increases project transparency. Further, as agile projects are open to change, it is possible, if needed, to replace a set of measures during the course of the process or to decide on different measure sets for different projects within the same organization. One general rule, however, should be followed: Measures should support and assist the individuals involved in the process.

8.2 Who Decides What Is Measured?

In an agile process, measures are determined by the customer, the team, and the organization management; each party decides what to measure based on its interests in the process and deliverables.

The customer is interested in measuring the progress and the quality of the deliverables, e.g., performances and stability; the team is interested in measuring the impacts of the methodology, the satisfaction of the people involved, and the quality of the artifacts from functional perspectives, such as maintainability and scalability; managerial people are interested in the business aspect, e.g., the project costs and return on investment, as well as customer satisfaction.

8.3 What Should Be Measured?

We measure artifacts that answer specific questions derived from specific goals. For example, suppose the team goal is to increase their productivity; questions that can be derived from this goal are as follows: How many hours per day teammates work to produce deliverables? How many hours per day teammates work in the collaborative workspace? What is the actual size of a work package? A measure set that helps answer such questions should fit the situation and the individuals. The set of measures should be refined and adapted when needed.

Measures should be as simple as possible to enable their actual measurement, as well as interpretation by the different stake holders participating in the process. For example, if teammates are requested to report every 15 min their time estimation for the remaining work, it will become annoying; instead, it can be decided to request it once a day.

Only several measures should be chosen; a large set of measures can influence negatively the process itself since many hours will be needed for the measurement process. Hence, a reasonable and refined set of measures should be used. This number of measures, however, should fit the team, the customer and the organization's needs. Our rule of thumb should be kept though: The tracker should invest no more than 20 % of his or her time for the collection, presentation, and refinement of the set of measures.

8.4 When Are Measures Taken?

The agile approach requires constant feedback. Therefore, there are activities, like continuous integration in software development projects, that should be measured several times each day. In such cases, it is preferable that the measures will be taken automatically. Other activities can be measured on a daily basis. For example, measures that reflect the number of hours invested each day in task performance and the hour distribution among the tasks completed during the day can be taken on a daily basis. Measurements taken on a daily or iteration basis allow ongoing reflection on the process progress as often as possible.

8.5 How Are Measures Taken?

Though there is a set of agreed upon measures, in order to foster and support measure collection, they are taken by the different roles assigned in the agile team. One measure that the tracker tracks compares the tasks' time estimation with their actual time; the quality assurance team is responsible, among other activities, for measures that deal with quality; the user evaluator is responsible for measures that reflect users' satisfaction with the user interface design and so on. The tracker is responsible, though, for the measure collection and their presentations.

8.6 Who Does Take Measure?

All team members are involved in measuring the progress, either by reporting essential information to the team members who are responsible for specific measures or by measure gathering, analysis, and presentation.

8.7 How Are Measures Used?

It is not sufficient to observe the measures on a regular basis in order to communicate the project status among the different individuals and stakeholders involved in the project. In addition to measure examination on a regular basis, after each period, preferable after each release that longs about 2–3 months, the mere information that the measures provide, together with their analysis, should be evaluated against the set of the projects goals. During such an iterative process, the goals and their subgoals are refined, the set of measures are determined and changed if needed, and the information is assessed to check its compliance with the current goals.

In the agile spirit, the conclusions derived from such an examination is communicated to all team members, the customer, and the management, whether by actual participation in such examination sessions or by other means found appropriate for a specific project setting.

8.8 Illustration for the Case of a Software Project

This section illustrates how measures are used for monitoring a large-scale project that the implementation of the agile approach for its development process was considered a risk (Talby et al. 2006). Specifically, we present two measures that were defined and deployed in this project.

Product size is the first measure. It aims at presenting the amount of completed work. The data selected to reflect the amount of the completed work is the number of test points. One test point is defined either as one test step in an automatic acceptance test scenario or as one line of unit tests. The total number of test points that passed successfully is calculated for each kind of test (either acceptance test or unit test) and is gathered per iteration per component. Additional information was gathered with respect to the number of test points for tests that passed, the number of test points for tests that failed, and the number of test points for tests that do not run at all. This product size measure was very effective in delivering the following message: Test points are the *only* measure that reflects the project productivity—nothing else counts.

The product size measure was designed to cope with the risk related to the inability to measure the project progress before the agile approach had been applied and, consequently, the inability to compare its current velocity (Beck and Fowler 2000; Cohn 2006) to that of the organization's previous development process. The advantage of test points, over, for example, the number of lines of code or lines of specifications, is that the number of test points for a given feature is usually proportional to the feature's size and complexity. This argument cannot be stated with respect to the number of lines of code or lines of specifications.

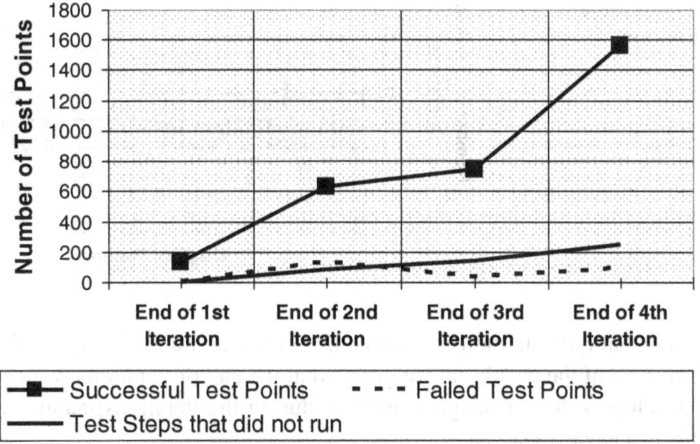

Fig. 8.1 Size measure during the release

Figure 8.1 shows a global view of the product size for one release (four iterations), reflecting the growing numbers of test points as the product development proceeded. The significant growth in the last iteration is explained by the relatively small number of testers' hours for automatic test writing that were allocated to the project at first and soon turned to be a bottleneck. In the third iteration, for example, not all coded features were tested, and accordingly, the size measure showed only a small increase. Consequently, it was decided that at the beginning of the fourth iteration, the main tester will teach the developers to write automatic test scenarios for their code. Accordingly, during the fourth iteration, she taught developers to write automatic tests, so she wrote fewer tests by herself. The result was a sharp increase in the product size measure during the fourth iteration.

Pulse is the second measure we present, which aims to measure the integration continuity. The data are automatically gathered from the development environment by counting on a daily basis the number of check-in operations. Data are gathered for code (together with its unit test) check-ins, automatic acceptance test check-ins, and detailed specifications check-ins.

The pulse measure was designed to monitor the risk of high overhead due to lack of continuous integration. Agile software development requires a different mind-set than the one that the practitioners in this project were used to: instead of completing a two-week specifications task and only then to start the development phase, when the agile approach started being implemented, an entire iteration was set to be two weeks long, during which a full cycle of specification–coding–testing is completed and usually more than one cycle per each teammate. When keeping a daily pulse constant, i.e., ongoing check-in integration of tested code, integration overhead and bug fixing are reduced.

Hence, the preliminary role of the pulse measure was to verify that integration is spread evenly across iterations. Accordingly, *steady* pulse is the desired status,

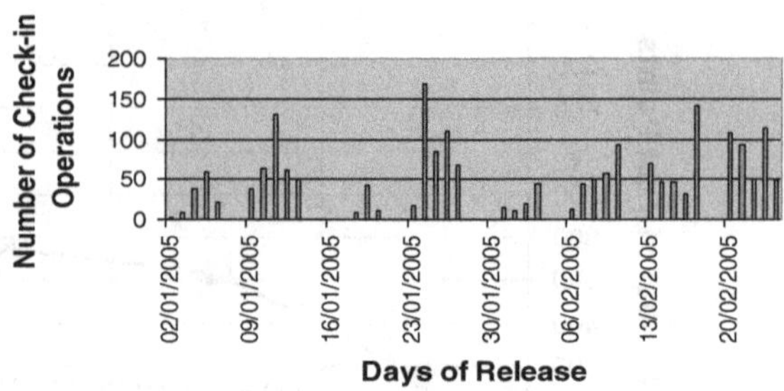

Fig. 8.2 Pulse measure during the release

and it means that pulse is more or less equal across the iteration days; *spiky* pulse means that most of the check-ins are grouped at the end of iterations, which means that the developers do not integrate enough during the iterations; naturally, spiky pulse reflects a negative signal.

Figure 8.2 shows the pulse measure for the entire release. As can be observed, the first week of each two-week iteration has fewer check-in operations than the second week of the iteration. Also, in the fourth iteration, the integration was distributed in the best way among the iteration days.

8.9 Summary

This chapter deals with measures that suit agile projects. Relevant goals and sub-goals are set, and measures are set accordingly. This approach ensures that measures are meaningful and provide a realistic way to add and/or remove measures according to their relevance.

References

Beck, K., Fowler, M.: Planning Extreme Programming. Addison-Wesley, Boston (2000)

Cohn, M.: Agile Estimating and Planning. In: Robert, C. Martin Series, Prentice Hall PTR (2006)

Dubinsky, Y., Yaeli, A., Feldman, Y., Zarpas, E., Nechushtai, G.: Governance of Software Development: The Transition to Agile Scenario, IT Governance and Service Management Frameworks and Adaptations, Section 3, Chapter XV. Idea Group Publishing, Information Science Publishing, IRM Press (2008)

Talby, D., Hazzan, O., Dubinsky, Y., Keren, A.: Agile SOFTWARE TESTING IN A LARGE-SCALE PROJECT. In: IEEE Software, Special Issue on Software Testing, pp. 30–37 (2006)

Chapter 9
Quality

Abstract High-quality assurance is a fundamental element of every project and is considered to be one of the difficult things to achieve and sustain. In this chapter, we describe how quality is perceived by the agile approach, addressing process and product quality. With respect to the process quality, we show how the transparency and tightness characteristics of the agile approach increase the process quality. For example, the iterative process performed in short iteration of 2–4 weeks increases the process tightness which, in turn, upsurges the process quality by enabling better control and faster response to unexpected problems and changes. With respect to the product quality, we elaborate on one of the agile practices that strongly related to software quality—test-driven development (TDD) (Beck et al. 2003; Feathers and Prentice Hall 2004; Newkirk and Vorontsov 2004; Mishali et al. 2008), which requires a collaborative development environment and additional supporting practices in order to be integrated successfully.

Keywords Quality · Process and product quality · Transparency · Tightness · Test-driven development (TDD) · Collaborative development environment

9.1 The Agile Approach to Quality

Agile projects eliminate the notion of 'production chain' in order to cope with problems associated with this notion. Instead, a more network-oriented structure, in which the quality assurance stage is intertwined alone the entire process, is advocated by the agile approach. Thus, all team members are equally responsible for the product quality during the *entire* project duration, and there is no passing on of responsibility to other entities in the organization.

Specifically, in the context of agile software projects, the term quality assurance does not appear as a specific stage of the development process. Table 9.1 compares the agile approach toward quality with some other approaches.

O. Hazzan and Y. Dubinsky, *Agile Anywhere*, SpringerBriefs in Computer Science,
DOI 10.1007/978-3-319-10157-6_9

Table 9.1 Some differences between agile and other methods with respect to quality

Quality-related aspect	The agile approach	Other approaches
Who is responsible for software quality?	All the development team members	The QA team
When are quality-related topics addressed?	All the time, quality is one of the primary concerns of the process	At the QA stage
Quality-related activities status	Same as other activities	Low (Cohen et al. 2004)
Work style	Collaboration with all parties	Developers and QA people may have conflicting interests

9.1.1 Process Quality

Transparency and tightness are two main characteristics of agile processes. These characteristics imply high-quality process, as is illustrated in what follows.

- The Business Day—allocated each two weeks for the presentation of the work accomplished in the previous iteration, reflective thinking, and planning of the next iteration—lays out a tight rhythm. This tightness guides a high-quality process since it controls the project management, among other ways, by enabling to reveal and deal with unexpected events at early stages.
- Planning sessions are performed when all project stakeholders present and all teammates hear the customer requirements. Consequently, project goals, subject, and features are known to everyone involved, and the project ongoing details are highly transparent. The impact of this transparency on quality is multifaceted. For example, it decreases misunderstandings and influences positively teammates' morale.
- Process measures, e.g., customer satisfaction and the project progress versus estimations, are available all the time to all people involved in the project, including the customer. The measurement process itself, as well as its ongoing availability to all project stakeholders, increases teammates' awareness, care, and attention to process quality issues.

9.1.2 Product Quality

There is no one standard way to measure product quality. In what follows we list two agile practices which aim at constantly improving product quality.

- *Refactoring* provides a simple and clear design which is easy to maintain and simplifies future extensions. When major needs for refactoring activities are recognized, refactoring tasks are formulated and are entered for consideration in the next planning session, to be presented to the customer and prioritized.

- *Acceptance tests* are defined by the teammates together with the customer in order to validate each customer's need. During the definition process of the acceptance tests, customer stories are elaborated and, consequently, their understanding is improved. The actual development of the acceptance tests increases teammates' confidence with respect to the correctness of the developed product and enables them to articulate the product functionality at the end of the iteration.

9.2 Test-Driven Development

Test-driven development (TDD) is an agile technique applied in agile projects that enables a step-by-step development of a specific functionality together with its unit tests, when each test step precedes its respective code step.

TDD aims to provide clean, fault-free code (Beck et al. 2003). In addition, refactoring activities further improve the code (Fowler 1999). Accordingly, the TDD guideline is red/green/refactor, where red means writing a simple test that fails; green means writing the minimal and simplest code that causes the test to pass; refactor means that code quality is improved without adding functionality. This guideline is iteratively implemented in small steps. The accumulative experience of the agile community is that TDD provides high-quality code (George and Williams 2003), which means that the code is readable and includes fewer bugs. In addition, through a TDD process, software developers improve their understanding with respect to the developed product (George and Williams 2004).

TDD can help overcome some of the common problems associated with traditional testing in software projects. Based on (Dubinsky and Hazzan 2007), the following TDD analysis addresses technical, cognitive, social, affective, and managerial facets and is structured around arguments frequently offered to explain why, in many cases, traditional testing is skipped. These arguments are accompanied by explanations on how TDD might help overcome these obstacles.

- *Not enough time to test*: Traditionally, unit testing, if exists, is performed after the code is written and usually under time pressure. According to Van Vliet (2000), "the testing activity often does not get the attention it deserves. By the time the software has been written, we are often pressed for time, which does not encourage thorough testing" (p. 397). However, "postponing test activities for too long is one of the most severe mistakes often made in software development projects. This postponement makes testing a rather costly affair" (ibid.). TDD eliminates this problem since unit tests are performed throughout the entire development process.
- *Testing provides negative feedback* : Traditional testing processes require developers to find bugs in their own work, and thus, testing activities end in failure. In TDD, the rules of the game are reversed. TDD ends in success: After a test fails, code is written and the test passes—success!

- *Responsibility for testing is transferred*: In some software development environments, bugs are found and fixed by other practitioners than the developer who wrote the code; thus, it is not clear who is responsible for each specific coding and testing activity. In TDD processes, the person who writes the code is also responsible for its testing.
- *Testing is a low-status job*: When testing is carried out at the end of the production line, inspired by traditional working class jobs, the task is attributed low status, which in turn leads to tension among different groups of employees (Cohen et al. 2004). Since in TDD processes, all developers test their own code; negative feelings toward testing and testers are eliminated.
- *Testing is hard to manage*: From a managerial perspective, it is sometimes claimed that testing slows down the development process. Since TDD is firmly integrated throughout the entire development process, it turns development and testing into controlled processes. Indeed, introducing TDD might slow down the development process in the short term simply because testing is actually performed. In the long run, however, it assists in shortening the integration period (especially when continuous integration is performed).
- *Testing is hard*: Testing is difficult mainly because it is not always clear what tests are suitable for a specific purpose and how much testing should be done. TDD as a detailed and explicit process improves one's understanding of what should be developed since the test is written prior to the writing of the code. Ron Jeffries explains the testing activity from the cognitive perspective: "A key aspect of this process do not try to implement two things at a time and do not try to fix two things at a time. Just do one. When you get this right, development turns into a very pleasant cycle of testing, seeing a simple thing to fix, fixing it, testing, and getting positive feedback all the way. Guaranteed flow"(http://c2.com/cgi/wiki?RonJeffries).

9.3 Summary

This chapter describes the agile approach to process and product quality. Specifically, it analyzes the implementation of test-driven development (TDD) from technical, cognitive, social, affective, and managerial perspectives.

References

Beck, K.: Test-driven development by example. Addison, Wesley (2003)

Cohen, C.F., Birkin, S.J., Garfield, M.J., Webb, H.W.: Managing conflict in software testing. Commun. ACM **47**(1), 76–81 (2004)

Dubinsky, Y., Hazzan, O.: Measured Test-Driven Development: Using Measures to Monitor and Control the Unit Development. J. Comput. Sci. Sci Publ. **3**(5), 335–344 (2007)

Feathers, M.: Working effectively with legacy code. Prentice Hall (2004)

Fowler, M.: Refactoring: improving the design of existing code. Addison-Wesley Professional (1999)

George, B., Williams, L.: An initial investigation of test driven development in industry. Proceedings of the ACM symposium on applied computing, pp. 09–12. Melbourne, Florida, Mar 2003

George, B., Williams, L.: A structured experiment of test-driven development. Inf. Softw. Technol. **46**, 337–342 (2004)

Mishali, O., Dubinsky. Y., Katz, S.: The TDD-guide training and guidance tool for test-driven development. International Conference on Agile Processes and Extreme Programming in Software Engineering (XP), Limerick, Ireland (2008)

Newkirk JW, Vorontsov AA (2004) Test-Driven Development in Microsoft .NET. Microsoft Press

Van Vliet, H.: Software Engineering—Principles and Practice. Wiley, NY (2000)

Chapter 10
Learning

Abstract The agile approach fits especially for projects whose final product is not entirely known at the project onset. Accordingly, a project development process can be viewed as a learning process both from the customers' and team members' perspectives. In such cases, on which we focus, at the beginning of the project, customers do not know explicitly and entirely what their requirements of the desired product are and improve their understanding with respect to these requirements during the project evolution process; team members keep improving their understanding of the customer requirements. Such processes require that an appropriate learning environment and atmosphere be provided to all project stakeholders. Indeed, this is another characteristic of agile environments—they inspire and support leaning processes. This chapter explores mechanisms that agile environments provide stakeholders of agile projects to support their learning processes.

Keywords Learning · Learning process · Project evolution · Customer requirements · Learning environment and atmosphere · Constructivism · Short releases and iterations

10.1 Agile Project from the Constructivist Perspective

Constructivism is a learning theory that examines the nature of learning processes. A central tenet of the constructivist approach is that learners construct new knowledge by rearranging and refining their existing knowledge. More specifically, according to the constructivist approach, new knowledge is constructed *gradually,* based on the learner's existing mental structures. Mental structures are developed in steps, each elaborating on preceding ones, though there may of course be regressions and blind alleys. This process is referred to by Leron and Hazzan (1997) as "learning by successive refinement" and it is closely related to the Piagetian mechanisms of assimilation and accommodation (Piaget 1977). The term *successive refinement* itself is borrowed from computer science, where

O. Hazzan and Y. Dubinsky, *Agile Anywhere*, SpringerBriefs in Computer Science,
DOI 10.1007/978-3-319-10157-6_10

it refers to a methodology that guides a gradual elaboration of complex programs (Dijkstra 1972). This use of successive refinements is based on the assumption that successive refinement is an especially effective way for the human mind, with its particular strengths and limitations, to deal with complexity.

In what follows we present one agile practice that supports gradual construction of knowledge. The discussion is placed on short releases and iterations, the focus of each one is determined by the customer who prioritizes the requirements and tasks according to his or her current preferences. It is shown how short releases and iterations lead to improved understanding of the developed product by the customer and team members and, consequently, they are able to carry out the product development more confidently.

We note that the attention to the importance of learning processes in product evolution has been increased in the past several years and is promoted also by other approaches, such as the *Lean Startup* (Ries 2011), which share with agility many common ideas. For example, one principle of the Lean Startup methodology is validated learning.

10.2 Short Releases and Iterations

It is a known fact that customers face difficulties in determining in advance all the required features of their desired product. In accordance with the practice of short iterations and releases, one mechanism that the agile approach uses to guide and support gradual understanding of the product requirements is Business Days, which include planning and reflective sessions and are conducted frequently. These planning sessions, and the reflective processes that accompanied them, provide the customers with the opportunity to rethink, refine, and improve their understanding of the product they require. Consequently, customers are able to define and communicate their requirements to the team members in a more precise and clear manner; at the same time, team members are continuously exposed to this improved sequence of articulations.

In addition, in each short iteration and release, the team members get feedback with respect to their understating so far of the customer's requirements. If they misunderstand a requirement, the customer can clarify his or her intentions; if they do not understand a specific customer request, they have the opportunity to clarify the customer's intention in a face-to-face interaction.

This kind of interaction is based on the realization that misunderstanding exists in understanding customer's requirements and that an opportunity to frequently improve and correct the understanding of what should be delivered, both by the customer and the team members, should be provided.

From the constructivist perspective, a project process that is based on short releases and iterations has several benefits connected to learning processes.

First, it allows both the customer and team members to focus on a relatively small portion of the deliverables;

Second, short releases and iterations do not require dealing with future requirements that are unknown at a specific stage and that will probably be clarified latter when the project evolvement proceeds;

Third, short iteration improves communication between the project stakeholders in general and between the customer and the team in particular. Specifically, the Business Day, which takes place after each short iteration and in which the customer, the team and management participate, enables all project stakeholders to gather, communicate, become familiar with the others' perspectives at the project, express their concerns with respect to process and the product, and reflect on previous stages. All these activities improve the understanding of the process and the product by all the project stakeholders as well as their decision-making processes;

Fourth, short iteration defines very clearly the time for feedback and reflective sessions, that is—at the end of each iteration. Consequently, it is clear to all project stakeholders that their learning process of the required product is constantly supported;

Fifth, in addition to the lessons learned during the reflective sessions that take place at the Business Day, the Business Days serve as a break that enables the practitioners to rest and detach for a while from the demanding, complex and tight process of agile project. When they return to their tasks for the next iteration, they may be able to exploit their cognitive and organizational capabilities more energetically;

Sixth, at the end of each iteration, the team presents to the customer what has been accomplished during the last iteration and if needed, shares with the customer misunderstandings and/or problems in the project evolution and deliverables. This practice clearly delivers the legitimacy of raising problems and solving them collectively. The contribution of these two activities—raising problems and solving them collectively—to learning processes can be explained by the constructivist perspective since mental models are shared, evaluated, discussed, and examined with respect to the problem at hand.

10.3 Summary

In this chapter, we focus on learning—a central element of projects whose final product is unknown at the project onset. From the constructivist perspective, we examined how the agile practice of short releases and iterations supports learning processes.

References

Dijkstra, E.W.: Notes on structured programming. In: Dahl, O.J., Hoare, C.A.R., Dijkstra, E.W. (eds.) Structured Programming. Academic Press, New-York (1972)

Leron, U., Hazzan, O.: Computers and applied constructivism. IFIP WG g.1. In: Working Conference—Secondary School Mathematics in the World of Communication Technologies:

Learning, Teaching and the Curriculum, pp. 195–203. Grenoble, France (The proceedings' title is: Information and Communications Technologies in School Mathematics) (1997)

Piaget, J.: Problems of equilibration. In: Appel M.H., Goldberg L.S. (eds.) Topics in Cognitive Development, vol. 1, Equilibration: Theory, Research and Application, pp. 3–13. Plenum Press, NY (1977)

Ries, E.: The lean startup: how today's entrepreneurs use continuous innovation to create radically successful businesses. Crown Business (2011)

Chapter 11
Abstraction

Abstract Abstraction is a cognitive means according to which, in order to overcome complexity at a specific stage of a problem-solving situation, we concentrate on the essential features of our subject of thought, ignoring irrelevant details (Devlin 2003; Kramer 2007). Abstraction is especially important in solving complex problems as it enables the problem solver to think in terms of conceptual ideas rather than in terms of their details. Though abstraction is a useful tool, it is not always used. Sometimes, it is just too difficult to think abstractly; in other cases, abstraction is not utilized due to lack of awareness to its significance and its potential contribution to problem-solving processes. This chapter describes how abstraction is expressed and encouraged in agile environments. Further, since abstraction can be addressed on different levels, the shift between different levels of abstraction can also support problem-solving processes. However, the knowledge of how and when to move between different levels of abstraction does not always come naturally, and requires some awareness. We discuss abstraction as it is manifested, either explicitly or implicitly, in agile environments in general and, for illustration, in software projects.

Keywords Abstraction · Cognition · Problem-solving situation · Agile environments · Customer stories · Level of abstraction · Agile projects

11.1 Abstraction Levels in Agile Projects

Based on Hazzan and Dubinsky (2003), we discuss abstraction as it is manifested, either explicitly or implicitly, in agile environments in general and, for illustration, in software projects. **Roles**. The role scheme applied by agile teams can be viewed as a means that guides software practitioners to look, to think, and to examine the development process on different levels of abstraction. More specifically, if a team

O. Hazzan and Y. Dubinsky, *Agile Anywhere*, SpringerBriefs in Computer Science,
DOI 10.1007/978-3-319-10157-6_11

member wishes to perform the personal role successfully, that is, to lead the project in the direction that the role specifies, he or she must gain a more global and abstract view at the developed product as well as at the development process; however, when working on a specific task, the role holder should think and work on a lower level of abstraction. Thus, the role holder gains two mental images of the project: one includes the details of a specific task and one encompasses a global view of a certain aspect of the project. These two perspectives improve the role holder's understanding of both the product and process, mutually support and complement each other, and, further, promote abstract thinking.

Planning. The planning sessions, which take place at Business Days at the end of each short iteration and release, direct the development process. They guide all project stakeholders to improve their understanding of the developed product gradually and periodically, partially by supporting a natural move between levels of abstraction. Specifically, while the release planning sessions inspire a global view on a higher abstraction level of the developed product, in the iteration planning sessions, planning is conducted on a lower level of abstraction, addressing the details of the development tasks for the next iteration as well as their time estimation.

Stand-up meeting. Stand-up meetings are conducted at the beginning of every day (or several days according to the project characteristics). Their goal is to share relevant information about the project as frequent as possible and to launch the working day(s). A stand-up meeting longs about 10 min in which each teammates describes, in his or her turn in up to 1 min, what he or she accomplished the previous day(s) with respect to the project development, what he or she is going to perform today, and main problems encountered, if exist. Teammates stand during the meeting to make it short and concise. On the individual level, the need to summarize previous and future activities requires each team member to take a more global and abstract view than the local detailed view needed during the actual working day; on the team level, the team gets an overview of the project status on a daily basis and may use these frequent statues reports to mentally construct an abstract image of the project.

Refactoring. Refactoring (Beck 2000; Fowler 1999; Highsmith 2002), or redesign, means that the software design is improved without adding functionality. Refactoring is based on the current design and it attempts to simplify it and ease the introduction of future changes.

Since the practice of refactoring encourages programmers to keep improving code structure and readability without adding functionality to the code, refactoring is a continuous and gradual process of code improvement. More specifically, since the final structure of the code and design cannot be predicted in advance, refactoring serves as a tool that leads and supports the team members in a gradual process of code and design improvement.

Refactoring is considered to be a complex cognitive activity that people face difficulties to accomplish. This difficulty can be explained by the need to think on the developed product on a high level of abstraction, which is considerably sophisticated than the level of abstraction on which code is written or designed.

The inclusion of refactoring as an agile practice delivers a clear message: it is legitimized to stop from time to time the development process of new tasks and to allocate time for code improvement. Further, in practice, when a need for an extensive refactoring is acknowledged, agreed upon, and approved by the customer, time is allocated for refactoring in the next iteration, and the same activities conduced with respect to code development, such as breaking down and time estimation, are conducted with respect to refactoring. As it turns out, the investment in refactoring, which results in clean, clear and easy-to-change code, is returned in future development and maintenance activities.

11.2 Summary

In this chapter, we focus on abstraction and present agile practices that guide abstract thinking in general and the transition between abstraction levels in particular. One of the main messages of this chapter is that the shift between levels of abstraction increases stakeholders' understanding of the project process and product.

References

Beck, K.: Extreme Programming Explained. Addison-Wesley, Boston (2000)

Devlin, K.: Why universities require computer science students to take math. Commun. ACM **46**(9), 37–39 (2003)

Fowler, M.: Refactoring—Improving the Design of Existing Code. Addison-Wesley, Boston (1999)

Hazzan, O., Dubinsky, Y.: Bridging cognitive and social chasms in software development using Extreme Programming. In: Proceedings of the Fourth International Conference on eXtreme Programming and Agile Processes in Software Engineering, Genova, Italy, pp. 47–53 (2003)

Hazzan, O., Kramer, J.: Abstraction in computer science and software engineering: a pedagogical perspective. Featured Frontier Columnist, System Design Frontier—Exclusive Frontier Coverage on System Designs **4**(1), 6–14 (2007)

Highsmith, J.: Agile Software Development Ecosystems. Addison Wesley (2002)

Kramer, J.: Is abstraction the key to computing? Commun. ACM **50**(4), 37–42 (2007)

Chapter 12
Trust

Abstract This chapter focuses on how trust is fostered by agility. The basic notion addressed in this chapter is the transparency of agile environments and how it increases trust among team members. Such an environment, in which trustful relationships exist, enhances ethical behavior and diversity. Relationships between agile processes, trust, ethics, and diversity are laid out in this chapter as well.

Keywords Trust · Transparency · Ethics · Ethical behavior · Diversity

12.1 Process Transparency

Project processes tend to be not transparent, especially in cases when the project deliverables are intangible, e.g., an assimilation project of a new medical regulation in a hospital or a development project of a new software application. Specifically, the project status is not always known, and it is not always clear if each team member has accomplished his or her tasks. Therefore, in such environments, it may be difficult to construct trust. This section illustrates how basic agile concepts increase project visibility, turning the project process to be more transparent (Hazzan 2007) and consequently foster trust among project stakeholders.

Short releases and iterations. The actual and detailed plan of the short releases and iterations is executed in Business Days, in which *all* relevant parties participate—customer, team members, management representatives, and so on. This activity, which usually takes about half a day, includes a presentation of what was developed in the previous iteration along with any relevant measures taken, a reflective session, and the planning of the next iteration. In the reflective session, the development process performed so far is analyzed and implications for the future are discussed and agreed upon. At the end of the day, a balanced workload is ensured among all team members. Clearly, the participation of all project stakeholders in this day, the nature of the activities that take place during the day, and the fact that it takes place every two weeks (or so), all increase the process visibility and make it more transparent.

O. Hazzan and Y. Dubinsky, *Agile Anywhere*, SpringerBriefs in Computer Science,
DOI 10.1007/978-3-319-10157-6_12

Time estimations. In agile environments, the teammate who is in charge of a specific task also estimates the time needed for its accomplishment. Not only teammate's responsibility to perform well is increased, but also this practice enhances process transparency since all teammates know what each practitioner has committed to in terms of time estimations.

Customer involvement. In agile environments, all team members have direct access to the customer during the entire project process. Clearly, this direct communication channel enhances both the process transparency and the chances that the product requirements are communicated correctly.

12.2 Ethics

Codes of ethics guide professionals how to behave in vague situations in which it is not clear what is right and what is wrong. The need for a code of ethics arises from the fact that any profession generates situations that can neither be predicted nor be answered uniformly by all members of the relevant professional community. In this section, we examine how agile environments foster ethical behavior in the case of software projects.

Many ethical issues are associated with information technologies, computing science and software engineering. To address this reality, the ACM/IEEE-CS Joint Task Force defined the Software Engineering Code of Ethics and Professional Practice (Version 5.2). Its short version is presented in what follows (for the full version look at http://www.acm.org/about/se-code).

The Software Engineering Code of Ethics and Professional Practice—Short Version[1]

Software Engineering Code of Ethics and Professional Practice
ACM/IEEE-CS Joint Task Force on Software Engineering Ethics and Professional Practices
Short Version
PREAMBLE

The short version of the code summarizes aspirations at a high level of the abstraction; the clauses that are included in the full version give examples and details of how these aspirations change the way we act as software engineering professionals. Without the aspirations, the details can become legalistic and tedious; without the details, the aspirations can become high sounding but empty; together, the aspirations and the details form a cohesive code.

Software engineers shall commit themselves to making the analysis, specification, design, development, testing, and maintenance of software a beneficial and respected profession. In accordance with their commitment to the health, safety, and welfare of the public, software engineers shall adhere to the following eight principles:

1. PUBLIC—Software engineers shall act consistently with the public interest.
2. CLIENT AND EMPLOYER—Software engineers shall act in a manner that is in the best interests of their client and employer consistent with the public interest.
3. PRODUCT—Software engineers shall ensure that their products and related modifications meet the highest professional standards possible.
4. JUDGMENT—Software engineers shall maintain integrity and independence in their professional judgment.
5. MANAGEMENT—Software engineering managers and leaders shall subscribe to and promote an ethical approach to the management of software development and maintenance.
6. PROFESSION—Software engineers shall advance the integrity and reputation of the profession consistent with the public interest.
7. COLLEAGUES—Software engineers shall be fair to and supportive of their colleagues.
8. SELF—Software engineers shall participate in lifelong learning regarding the practice of their profession and shall promote an ethical approach to the practice of the profession.

We review two sections of the above code of ethics from the perspective of agility.

2. CLIENT AND EMPLOYER—Software engineers shall act in a manner that is in the best interests of their client and employer consistent with the public interest.

This section of the code of ethics is fostered by agile processes by the close interaction between the team members and the customer. Specifically, the facts that the customer is in close interaction with the team and that all project stakeholders hear the customers' requirements further support the enhancement of this section of the code of ethics.

4. JUDGMENT—Software engineers shall maintain integrity and independence in their professional judgment.

Integrity is maintained in agile environments by encouraging agile team members to raise problem they encounter to discuss dilemmas, and to express their concerns. Several opportunities are provided to agile team members for such articulations, such as reflective sessions and stand-up meetings.

In general, since agile processes are transparent, ethical behavior is encouraged and fostered. This is because behaviors are more seeable and consequently, ethical behavior is more easily accepted, and norms can be set and adhered.

12.3 Diversity

Diversity can be expressed in different ways, such as nationalities, genders, minorities, cultures, and lifestyles. Diversity can also be expressed with respect to internal characteristics, such as worldviews, hobbies, skills, and thinking styles.

In general, studies tell us that no matter how diversity is expressed, it benefits and enhances societies that foster it (e.g., Florida 2002, Hazzan and Dubinsky 2006). Diversity is also perceived as a powerful managerial practice (Thomas 2004) due to its added value to problem-solving processes and the need to address international markets.

At the same time, however, and mainly with respect to social and ethnic diversity, resistance is sometimes expressed toward diversity. The main argument presented is that people tend not to trust people who are different than them (e.g., Smith 2001, 2007). According to (Austin 1997), "there may be an optimal level of diversity that will stimulate creative thinking within a group, and the relationship between group diversity and creativity may be curvilinear" (p. 342). Accordingly, Austin suggests that organizations increase their awareness to disagreements that may stem from diversity.

So far, we saw how the transparent nature of agile environments fosters trust and ethical norms. Within such conditions, diversity can also flourish. This is because when trust is increased, team members are more open to new ideas and perspectives in general and to diversity in particular.

Specifically, diversity is enhanced in agile environments in several ways. For example, the role scheme enables each team member to express his or her perspective at the process and product and to influence both of them; the participation of all project stakeholders in the planning sessions, as well as in the reflective sessions, enhances the contribution and expression of different opinions.

In turn, agile teams may benefit from this enhanced diversity in several ways.

First, the more diverse a team is, the more wide-ranging perspectives are elicited; consequently, teammates are exposed to others' perspectives and are able to use these different points of view in different new (problem-solving) situations.

Second, the project deliverable itself may be improved because when different perspectives are expressed with respect to a specific aspect of the deliverable, the chances that subtle issues will emerge are higher; consequently, additional factors are considered when decisions related to the said deliverable are taken.

Third, the entire process is more questioned when diverse opinions are expressed, and once again, the team may get a more argument-based process.

Fourth, diversity reduces resistance to new ideas and establishes an open atmosphere toward alternative opinions.

Finally, since more and more companies become global, diversity is becoming an integral characteristic of teams and, therefore, cannot be neglected. It is just natural to assume that a team, which welcomes diversity, may assimilate its behavior in this global market more naturally and successfully.

12.4 Summary

This chapter binds ethics and diversity under the notion of trust. It is explained how agile environments increase trust by establishing a transparent environment. In this transparent environment, ethical behavior and diversity can flourish and, in turn, foster back and enhance the agile process and the evolved product.

References

Austin, JR.: A cognitive framework for understanding demographic influences in groups. Int. J. Organ. Anal. **5**(4) 342–359 (1997)

Florida, R.: The rise of the creative class. Basic Books, New York (2002)

Hazzan, O.: Agile software development and the nature of software development. Featured Front. Columnist, Syst. Des. Front—Exclusive Front. Coverage Syst. Des. **4**(3), 28–32 (2007)

Hazzan, O., Dubinsky, Y.: Can diversity in global software development be enhanced by agile software development? In: Proceedings of the International Conference of Software Engineering, ICSE, International Workshop on Global Software Development for the Practitioner (GSD), Shanghai, China (2006)

Smith, MK.: 'Robert Putnam', the encyclopedia of informal education. www.infed.org/thinkers/putnam.htm. Last update: November 05, 2007 (2001, 2007)

Thomas, D.: Diversity as strategy. Harvard Business Review 98-108 http://www.gpworldwide.com/quick/sep2004/art2.asp (2004)

References

Chapter 13
Globalization

Abstract Globalization is usually related to time, distance, and culture. Referring to time, we cite Friedman's book *The World is Flat*: "… That's globalization, said Nilekani. Above the screen, there were eight clocks that pretty well summed up the Infosys workday: 24/7/365. The clocks were labeled US West, US East, GMT, India, Singapore, Hong Kong, Japan, Australia" (Friedman 2005, p. 6). Referring to distance, a physical distance between teams, which work together on one product, increases the process complexity. It is further claimed that even a 50 m distance can be considered as a distributed environment (Allen 1984 in Sangwan et al. 2007). Referring to culture, this concept has been explored extensively with respect to different kinds and sizes of groups like nations, tribes, and teams. We define the concept of culture as a set of explicit and implicit norms, values, and beliefs, shared by the practitioners in a group to which they belong that, on one hand, influences directly the practitioners' daily activities, behaviors, and interactions and, on the other hand, is fed back by these activities, behaviors, and interactions and is shaped by them. The culture of a specific team is influenced by the culture of the nation as well as the organizational culture. Both are relevant for global environments. In this chapter, we address globalization as it is expressed by agile teams.

Keywords Globalization · Global product development · Time, distance, and culture · Process complexity · Values and beliefs · Agile teams · Software projects · Development methodology

13.1 Agile Global Product Development

Global software development refers to distributed teams which work together on one product development (Carmel et al. 2010; Herbsleb et al. 2001; Sahay et al. 2003; Sangwan et al. 2007). The motivation for such setting usually stems from

O. Hazzan and Y. Dubinsky, *Agile Anywhere*, SpringerBriefs in Computer Science,
DOI 10.1007/978-3-319-10157-6_13

the need to use the organization resources cost-competitively and the need to shorten time to market by "around-the-clock" development.

The following description is our expansion of "agile global and distributed *software* development" to "agile global and distributed *product* development," which delivers the message that agility can be applied also to other distributed projects, not necessarily software. Since the developed product of distributed teams includes also its delivery between the project sites, it seems that the description fits especially the development of intangible products that can be delivered electronically between the project sites to enable "around-the-clock" progress.

In general, agile distributed teams adhere to the notion of communication by (a) setting the resources and procedures needed for fruitful communication, including its tracking, and (b) deciding on communication facilitator, channels, and measures. Specifically, Sangwan et al. (2007) suggested that the communication among distributed teams should be adequate, not too minor and not overwhelmed and, in any case, should be measured.

Teams should be synchronized in order to develop a high-quality product, and therefore, in distributed teams, the planning activity serves also for coordination and synchronization purposes. Different techniques and tools are suggested for the planning activity of projects developed in distributed environments. Cusick and Prasad (2006) present some recommendations, emerged from the experiences with many global non-agile projects that fit also agile environments as well. For example, "Limit phase durations to keep control. Shorter phases are easier to track and manage. Track all issues assiduously. Require interim deliveries to ensure quality."

Reflection is also one of the most important tools to control and improve performances in distributed environments. It provides teammates with a medium to talk about problems and discuss main concerns. Further, it highlights information about the process and enables to accommodate improvements in order to reduce some of the frustration felt sometimes by practitioners in distributed environments.

13.2 Software Projects and Culture

Connections between software development methods and cultural issues have been discussed (Yourdon 1997; Sawyer and Guinan 1998). For example, according to Moore (2000), there are four basic organizational cultures: cultivation, competence, collaboration, and control, to which he matches one of three methodology categories: rigorous (RM), agile (AM), or ad hoc or no methodology (NM).

A cultivation culture is motivated by self-realization and can be illustrated by Silicon Valley start-up companies, to which fits the NM category. *Lean Start-up* (Ries 2011) is a more recent methodology, which shares with agility many common ideas, and has been designed especially for coping with challenges that characterize start-ups companies.

A competence culture is driven by the need for achievement; collaboration cultures are driven by a need for affiliation, and control cultures are motivated by the need for power and security. Naturally, the agile approach fits the competence and the collaboration cultures, and the RM fits the control culture.

Highsmith (2002) adds another dimension and associates each methodology to a specific product development phase. According to Highsmith, while the NM approach fits the initial phases of product development, at later stages, when close interaction with customers is required, the AM approach fits better. During the main street market phase, the RM approach fits in the best.

13.3 Summary

This chapter focuses on globalization and agile distributed team. We suggest that the agile approach fits global development due to its visibility, transparency, and tightness characteristics that contribute to colocated teams and, therefore, maybe furthermore, fits for distributed ones. We also address relationships between development processes and the notion of culture.

References

Allen, T.J.: Managing the Flow of Technology: Technology Transfer and the Dissemination of Technological Information within the R&D Organization. MIT Press, Cambridge (1984)

Carmel, E., Espinosa, J.A., Dubinsky, Y.: "Follow the sun" workflow in global software development. J. Manage. Inf. Syst. (JMIS) **27**(1), 17–38 (2010)

Cusick, J., Prasad, A.: A practical management and engineering approach to offshore collaboration. IEEE Softw. **5**, 20–29 (2006)

Friedman, T.L.: The World is Flat: A Brief History of the Twenty-First Century. Farrar, Straus and Giroux (2005)

Herbsleb, J.D., Mockus, A., Finholt, T.A., Grinter, R.: An Empirical Study of Global Software Development: Distance and Speed. In: Proceedings of the 23th international conference on software engineering (ICSE), IEEE Computer Society Press, Los Alamitos, CA (2001)

Highsmith, J.: Agile Software Developments Ecosystems. Addison-Wesley, MA (2002)

Moore, G.A.: Living on the Fault Line: Managing For Shareholder Value in the Age of The Internet. HarperBusiness, New York (2000)

Ries, E.: The Lean Startup: How Today's Entrepreneurs Use Continuous Innovation To Create Radically Successful Businesses. Crown Business (2011)

Sahay, S., Nicholson, B., Krishna, S.: Global IT Outsourcing: Software Development Across Borders. Cambridge University Press, Cambridge (2003)

Sangwan, R., Bass, M., Mullick, N., Paulish, D.J., Kazmeier, J.: Global Software Development Handbook. AuerBach Publications, Taylor and Francis Group, London (2007)

Sawyer, S., Guinan, P.J.: Software development: processes and performance. IBM Syst. J. **37**(4), http://www.research.ibm.com/journal/sj/374/sawyer.html (1998)

Yourdon, E.: Death March: The Complete Software Developer's Guide to Surviving "Mission Impossible" Projects. Prentice Hall PTR, NJ (1997)

Chapter 14
Reflection

Abstract Reflective thinking is a skill used by people in different situations. It is especially valuable in general-purpose projects, in learning processes, and definitely in complex development processes (Schön 1987; Hazzan 2002). This chapter focuses on the nature of reflective processes in agile environments on the individual level (reflection) and on the team level (retrospective). While reflection provides the individuals feedback with respect to how they perceive different aspects of the process and product, retrospective elevates these thoughts to the team level.

Keywords Reflection · Reflective thinking · Reflective processes · Agile environments · Retrospective · Retrospective session · Reflective practitioner perspective · Retrospective facilitator · Whole team · Trigger

14.1 Reflective Practitioner Perspective

Reflection is the process according to which an individual examines his or her actions during the accomplishment of a task or after the task has been accomplished. Though reflection is not a new concept, its common practice has been boosted after Schön had published his two books *The Reflective Practitioner* in 1983 and *Educating the Reflective Practitioner* in 1987 (Schön 1983, 1987). In order to become a reflective practitioner, one should keep reflecting on his or her accomplishments, activities, and behaviors. Schön's books advocate the idea that a person who keeps reflecting becomes a reflective practitioner, a position which enables him or her to keep improving his or her professional skills.

Generally speaking, the reflective practitioner perspective (Schön 1983, 1987) guides professional practitioners (such as architects, managers, musicians, and others) toward examining and rethinking their professional creations during and after the accomplishment of the process of creation. The working assumption is that such a reflection improves both proficiency and performance within such

O. Hazzan and Y. Dubinsky, *Agile Anywhere*, SpringerBriefs in Computer Science,
DOI 10.1007/978-3-319-10157-6_14

professions. Analysis of the agile approach supports the adoption of the reflective practitioner perspective to software engineering processes (Hazzan 2002; Hazzan and Tomayko 2003). Specifically, a reflective mode of thinking may improve the performance of some of the agile practices.

Though the importance of reflective processes is acknowledged by many professions, it is not always done if time is not specifically allocated and dedicated for this process. Accordingly, since the agile approach acknowledges the importance of reflective processes, it allocates specific time slots for their accomplishments. One time slot is a retrospective that usually takes place at the end of the release.

14.2 Retrospective

Retrospective is a reflective session that takes place on the team level, usually during long sessions (from 1 h to several days). In retrospectives, in addition to personal reflective processes, the team, as a whole, facilitates reflective thinking to derive lessons from its past experience.

Though the concept of retrospective usually refers to long sessions that take place at the end of the release, we adopt this notion for any *team* gathering (such as the end of the iteration meetings) whose aim is to reflect on the team performances in order to improve the process and product. We note that the term team may encompass also, if needed, the customer, the management, and other project stakeholders.

In retrospective sessions, each team member shares his or her reflection with the other participants in order to improve the team performances, and consequently, the process and product quality. Accordingly, communication and feedback are important in retrospective sessions and should be enhanced.

Since other kinds of tasks are not accomplished during the retrospective session, the mere existence of retrospective sessions delivers a clear message about their importance. This message is based on the anticipated contribution of the retrospective sessions to future performances and to the product and process quality. In other words, it is assumed that the invested time in the retrospective sessions is returned in improved product and process quality.

14.3 The Retrospective Facilitator

Each retrospective session should be facilitated by a moderator. One option is to invite a facilitator who is not part of the team. Another option is to assign one of the team members to be the retrospective facilitator. Teams which facilitate retrospective session on a regular basis can either add the role of retrospective facilitator to the role scheme, or add this responsibility to one of the other roles in the team. Alternatively, the retrospective facilitator role can be rotated between the team members. It is recommended that the retrospective facilitator knows how to facilitate retrospective processes; nevertheless, even if none of the team members is familiar with guiding retrospective processes, the team can dedicate the needed time for a gradual improvement of its retrospective sessions in the spirit of constructivism.

The role of the retrospective facilitator includes the selection of a subject for the retrospective, in coordination with the team leader, and the actual facilitation (including time keeping) of the retrospective meeting itself. During the retrospective, the facilitator should give special attention to the fact that all the participants are active and highly communicative.

14.4 Guidelines for a Retrospective Session

The following guidelines were formulated by a software team for its retrospective sessions that take place at each of its Business Days (Talby et al. 2006).

- Only one specific problem is discussed at each retrospective meeting.
- The discussed problem should relate to the project process, less to its product.
- The subject is chosen in advance by the moderator (after informal/formal consultation with other team members) and presented at the beginning of the retrospective meeting.
- The retrospective does not exceed 1 h.
- The whole team is required to attend the retrospective.
- Everyone is proactively encouraged to speak, but is not required to do so.
- Team members are encouraged to speak their own opinions.
- The moderator records important insights and proposes action items that surface during the meeting.
- The moderator publishes the main insights and action items to the team soon after the retrospective.
- The decided action items are applied immediately; these are changes in the day-to-day team operations that should reduce the debated problem, if exists.

14.5 Application of Agile Practices in Retrospective Sessions

This section presents several facilitation guidelines for retrospective sessions in agile environments. These guidelines deliver the message that when a retrospective session takes place in an agile project, the retrospective itself should also be performed in the spirit of agility, and accordingly, for example, it should foster diversity, support learning processes, and include the whole team, as is illustrated in what follows.

Time allocation As with other activities, time should be allocated for the retrospective session as well.

Whole team Everyone who belongs to the team should participate in the retrospective. Also, it is recommended that the team will take an active part in the preparation of the retrospective as well as during it and after it, when the decided upon lessons are implemented.
Abstraction During the retrospective meeting, it is recommended to address the discussed topics on different levels of abstraction—from conceptual ideas to practical activities and measures—and vise versa. Further, it is recommended to highlight this movement between abstraction levels to enable the participants exploit also cognitive benefits from this mental activity.
Measures It is important to accompany the application of each decision made in a retrospective session by a measure that, first, will enable to observe whether or not the decision itself is applicable, and second, to examine its actual performance and contribution to the process.

14.6 End of the Release Retrospective

This section suggests a framework for the end-of-the-release retrospective. The framework should be adjusted for each specific team's and project's needs. For additional details about the facilitation of retrospective session with software teams, see Kerth's book *Project Retrospective* (Kerth 2001).
Place It is recommended to facilitate the release retrospective out of the project site. The idea behind this recommendation is to disconnect the practitioners from their ongoing work in order to enhance reflective thinking and to deliver the message that the retrospective is important at least as the direct work on the product itself. This importance is highlighted by allocating a special time and place framework for the retrospective session, as is done for other kinds of tasks.
Length For a retrospective that takes place at the end of the release, in which the team wishes to get a comprehensive picture and understanding of the release, a longer period of time should be allocated. The longer period of time gives the team a time-out before the next release starts. Therefore, two days seem to be an optimal period.
Participants The retrospective participants should be determined according to the retrospective's target, team climate and dynamics, the project stage, and the lessons learned in previous retrospective sessions. When a specific decision is made with respect to the group of participation, its rational should be shared with all project stakeholders.
Topic(s) In order to address most of the team members' concerns in the retrospective, it is recommended to select the retrospective subject(s) a priori from a list generated by the team and is accessible to everyone. Such topic selection process has several advantages. First, the subject is relevant for at least several team members; second, it is reasonable to assume that a topic selected in this way

would be connected to the daily project life; third, time is not spent in the retrospective meeting to decide on the subject on which the retrospective will focus; fourth, such a selection process increases the environments transparency. Yet, in some cases, the team leader or a project manager may suggest topics which were not selected democratically. From the suggested list of topics, it is recommended to select topics that different opinions have been expressed with respect to them and to avoid the selection of a topic that involves personal quarrels and accusations.

Preparation The participants should be encouraged to bring to the retrospective session ideas, event descriptions, measures, and personal stories related to the retrospective topics.

To encourage the participants to start preparing themselves to the retrospective, they can be invited to bring into the retrospective one positive experience they experienced during the release and one experience they have bad feeling about. The retrospective facilitator, on his or her side, should be aware of the different concerns that the practitioners bring into the retrospective.

Global planning should be constructed accordingly; yet, some freedom level should be left to enable the accommodation of the retrospective timetable according to participants' needs and unexpected events that may come up in the retrospective.

Organization As in agile processes, it is recommended to base the retrospective session on cycles, each of them includes a trigger (explained bellow), a group activity, a discussion, and a summary.

If the retrospective participants break into subgroups for different activities, the subgroups' members should be modified for each activity in order to allow all the retrospective participants interact with as many other participants as possible. The gathering of all the retrospective participants after group activities, in which the groups report on their conclusion to the entire retrospective milieu and a discussion is facilitated, is an important element and should not be skipped.

Trigger A trigger is a means that fosters thinking on open topics. A well-selected trigger can open the participants' horizons to new ideas and enable them to communicate their ideas with respect to the discussed topics from new perspectives. There are different kinds of triggers. Since they vary in the time it takes to facilitate them, the retrospective facilitator should select them according to the target of the retrospective and the available time. Among many options, movies can serve as triggers. For example, a movie about a leader or about a natural phenomenon can serve as a trigger that stimulates interesting discussions. After the movie is watched, similarities and differences between what is seen in the movie (that is taken from another world) and what happens in the project environment can be discussed. This is of course only one option. Movies are good triggers for retrospective sessions since they encourage diversity by enabling each team member to think and connect what he or she watches to his or her personal and professional life experience.

14.7 Summary

This chapter looks at the contribution of reflective processes—reflection and retrospective—to agile processes. We emphasize that these practices should be addressed as other kinds of tasks are treated in agile environments, that is, with specific time allocation and the application of agile practices.

References

Hazzan, O.: The reflective practitioner perspective in software engineering education. J. Syst. Softw. **63**(3), 161–171 (2002)

Hazzan, O., Tomayko, J.: The reflective practitioner perspective in eXtreme programming. In: Proceedings of XP Agile Universe, New Orleans, Louisiana, USA 51–61 (2003)

Kerth, N.L.: Project Retrospectives: A Handbook for Team Reviews. Dorset House Publishing Company, New York (2001)

Schön, D.A.: The Reflective Practitioner. Basic Books, New York (1983)

Schön, D.A.: Educating the Reflective Practitioner: Towards a New Design for Teaching and Learning in The Profession. Jossey-Bass, San Francisco (1987)

Talby, D., Hazzan, O., Dubinsky, Y., Keren, A.: Reflections on reflection in agile software development. In: Proceedings of the Agile Conference, Minneapolis, Minnesota, USA 100–110 (2006)